success

Improve Your Communication Skills

CREATING SUCCESS

With over 1 million copies sold in over 30 languages, the Creating Success series covers 13 key skills and features bestselling authors Michael Armstrong and John Adair.

Dealing with Difficult People
Roy Lilley

How to Manage People
Michael Armstrong

Improve Your Communication Skills
Alan Barker

Taking Minutes of Meetings
Joanna Gutmann

How to Write a Business Plan
Brian Finch

How to Organize Yourself
John Caunt

Develop Your Leadership Skills
John Adair

How to Write Reports and Proposals
Patrick Forsyth

Decision Making and Problem Solving
John Adair

Develop Your Presentation Skills
Theo Theobald

Successful Project Management
Trevor L Young

Successful Time Management
Patrick Forsyth

How to Write a Marketing Plan
John Westwood

creating success
OVER 1 MILLION COPIES SOLD

@KPEmployability

www.koganpage.com/creating-success

KoganPage

creating
success

Improve Your Communication Skills

Alan Barker

KoganPage

First published in Great Britain and the United States in 2000 by Kogan Page Limited
Second edition 2006
Third edition 2013
Fourth edition 2016

2nd Floor, 45 Gee Street	122 W 27th St	4737/23 Ansari Road
London	10th Floor	Daryaganj
EC1V 3RS	New York NY 10001	New Delhi 110002
United Kingdom	USA	India

© Alan Barker, 2000, 2006, 2013, 2016

ISBN   978 0 7494 7575 8
E-ISBN   978 0 7494 7576 5

British Library Cataloguing-in-Publication Data

A CIP record for this book is available from the British Library.

Library of Congress Cataloging-in-Publication Data

Names: Barker, Alan, 1956- author.
Title: Improve your communication skills / Alan Barker.
Description: Fourth edition. | New York, NY : Kogan Page, 2016. | Series:
   Creating success | Revised edition of Improve your communication skills,
   2013.
Identifiers: LCCN 2016025738 (print) | LCCN 2016034252 (ebook) | ISBN
   9780749475758 (paperback) | ISBN 9780749475765 (ebook)
Subjects: LCSH: Business communication. | BISAC: BUSINESS & ECONOMICS /
   Careers / General. | BUSINESS & ECONOMICS / Business Communication /
   General. | SELF-HELP / Personal Growth / General.
Classification: LCC HF5718 .B365 2016 (print) | LCC HF5718 (ebook) | DDC
   651.7–dc23
LC record available at https://lccn.loc.gov/2016025738

Typeset by Graphicraft Limited, Hong Kong
Print production managed by Jellyfish
Printed and bound by CPI Group (UK) Ltd, Croydon CR0 4YY

Contents

About this book

It's official. Being able to communicate well sets you apart from the crowd. In 2014, the Graduate Management Admission Council asked nearly 600 employers what skills they most looked for in new recruits. Communication skills headed the list: organizations ranked them, on average, twice as important as managerial skills. And of the top four skills, the highest ranking were speaking and listening.

Why do these skills matter so much?

Partly because command-and-control structures are no longer in vogue. In these days of project and matrix management, we need to be able to influence each other without the armour of managerial authority.

The wider work environment is also changing. The boundaries between specialisms and professions are breaking down. As we outsource and set up strategic partnerships, we need to build effective relationships with customers, suppliers and other stakeholders. Work is increasingly becoming a network of conversations.

And yet the quality of our speaking and listening has never been more threatened. We're busier than ever; as we struggle to manage information overload, workplace conversations are often reduced to bulleted 'to-do' lists. Open-plan offices offer no privacy; if we want a quiet, informal chat, we must scuttle out to the nearest café. And technology is altering the way we communicate, in ways we're only beginning to understand. What is certain is that we're conversing less and writing more: texts, e-mails, tweets. We look at screens, some of us, more than we look at each other.

We desperately need to rediscover the skills of speaking and listening. In the employers' survey mentioned above, the other two highly rated communication skills – presenting and writing – both relate to conversation. If we can hold better conversations, then our presentations, e-mails and reports will all benefit.

That is why this book covers all four of those communication skills. Speaking, listening, presenting and writing: master those skills and you will be well placed to win the job you want, and forge a career that you can be proud of.

1 What is communication?

How would you define the word 'communication'? It is a question I often ask at the start of training courses. So let me ask you the same question.

EXERCISE

Complete this sentence in no more than 12 words:

Communication is...

Ask a few colleagues for their ideas. Compare your thoughts. Are you defining communication in all its forms? Are you defining effective communication? What makes communication ineffective? Can you agree on a definition?

The transmission model

In the 19th century, the word 'communication' referred mainly to the movement of goods and people. We still use the word in this way, of course: roads and railways are forms of communication, just as much as speaking or writing. And we still use industrial images as metaphors for communication. Information, like freight, needs to be stored, transferred and retrieved. And we often describe the movement of information in terms of a 'channel', along which information 'flows'.

In the 20th century, this transport metaphor readily adapted itself to the new, electronic technologies: we have 'telephone lines' and 'television channels'. Electronic information comes in 'bits', stored in 'files' or 'vaults'. The words 'download' and 'upload' use the freight metaphor; e-mail uses postal imagery.

So it wouldn't be surprising, in that exercise just now, if you defined communication as 'the effective transfer of information'. After all, what do we do when we communicate? We 'have' an idea (as if the idea were an object). We 'put the idea into words' (like putting it into a box); we try to 'put our idea across' (by pushing it or 'conveying' it); and the 'receiver' – hopefully – 'gets' the idea. We may need to 'unpack' the idea before the receiver can fully 'grasp' it. Of course, we need to be careful to avoid 'information overload'.

This is the transmission model of communication. And it is very attractive. It suggests that information is objective – something that both the transmitter and receiver will understand in the same way – and measurable (how many bits are we transmitting?). Above all, the model is simple: we can draw a diagram to illustrate it.

But does the transmission model reflect what actually happens when people communicate?

From transmission to reception: turning the model around

So what is wrong with the transmission model?

Well, to begin with, a message differs from a parcel in a very obvious way. When I send a parcel, I no longer have it; when I send a message, I still have it. But there is a more serious reason why the model fails to describe communication accurately. The model is the wrong way around.

Here's the first and most important point to make about communication: communication begins not with transmission, but with reception.

No matter how effectively I transmit information, it will not communicate to you if you don't receive it. And in order to receive it, you have to do three things:

- You have to pay attention.
- You have to understand.
- You have to put what you understand in context.

You could say that these are the three most basic communication skills.

Paying attention

Whatever you notice has the potential to communicate with you:

- If you notice a sign warning you about a bend in the road, you can adjust your driving.
- If you notice a loud siren that suddenly blares through the office, you can evacuate the building.
- If I say to you, 'Once upon a time', you will make yourself ready to hear a story.

But of course, we often notice things that are not intended to communicate to us. We notice the rabbit running out in front of the car, or our colleagues leaping out of their chairs as the siren rings, or the slow, low music of the storyteller's voice. All of these things will communicate if we notice them.

Communication begins, not with the intention to communicate, but with the act of paying attention.

How we understand

Of course, paying attention is not sufficient for communication to happen. We also need to understand what we are attending to. So how do we understand?

Essentially, understanding is a pattern-matching process. We create meaning by matching what our senses pick up to mental patterns inside our brains.

Let's look at those three examples again:

- That sign on the road would mean nothing to you if you didn't have a mental pattern of that sign already in your head. You learnt that sign, either by reading a manual or by asking people around you.

- Similarly, you know that sudden loud sounds usually signal danger. In this case, the mental pattern is probably imprinted genetically in your brain: all hearing animals will react violently to sudden, loud sounds.

- And those mesmerizing rhythms in the storyteller's voice activate mental patterns, probably below the level of consciousness. They prime you for the sequence of events that make the story gripping.

Understanding, then, is an active process. We provide the mental patterns that complete the information and give it meaning. As Stephen Jay Gould famously said: 'The mind, basically, is a pattern-seeking machine.'

Sometimes, the mental pattern-matching is simple. A road sign, for example, is designed to deliver a clear message. But, very often, we are working with information that is incomplete, garbled or ambiguous. And on those occasions, we have to fill in the gaps.

Take a look at the image in Figure 1.1:

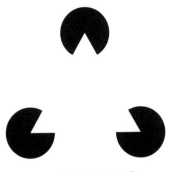

FIGURE 1.1 A Kanizsa triangle

What can you see? My guess is that you can see a white triangle. Of course, there is no white triangle; your brain has filled in the gaps. It has matched the available information to its store of mental patterns, and come up with the best guess of a white triangle. (The triangle is named after Gaetano Kanizsa, an Italian psychologist and artist, founder of the Institute of Psychology of Trieste.)

Scientists call this process of filling in the gaps 'perceptual completion', and it is not limited to visual information. Perceptual completion shows that everything we understand is a best guess of what is there.

Putting it all in context

Because all understanding is a best guess, most of us have become very good at guessing what information means.

The key to this skill is being able to read context. That loud siren in the office might be an emergency; but you've probably learned that it often sounds as a test, and sometimes by mistake. Understanding the context when you hear the siren helps you decide whether or not to head for the fire exit.

Context affects the way we understand each other, too. Imagine that we greet each other and I ask: 'How are you?' You answer: 'I'm fine.' Those two words could convey any one of these ideas:

- 'I'm feeling well.'
- 'I'm happy.'
- 'I was feeling unwell but am now feeling better.'
- 'I was feeling unhappy but now feel less unhappy.'
- 'I'm not injured; there's no need to help me.'
- 'Actually, I feel lousy but I don't want you to know it.'
- 'Help!'

How will I decide what you mean? What will I notice?

In a simple interchange like this, I would guess what you mean from the context in which you say those two words. I would register the tone, speed and volume of your voice; your facial expression; your gestures; and your posture. (Psychologists call this paralinguistic information: the information surrounding the words.) I might also think about the history of our friendship, the situation in which we meet, our cultural background and so on.

And even then, what I understand will still only be a best guess. To understand more accurately, I would need to ask you questions. We would need to continue the conversation.

Getting to know each other

In that simple exchange we looked at just now, how could you help me to understand your answer more clearly?

To begin with, you could ask yourself:

'What effect am I having?'

Let's pause here for a moment and think about that question.

What effect am I having on the other person?

If you want to improve your communication skills, I think that this is just about the most important and useful question you can ask yourself. The effect we have on another person is what we communicate to them. It is an incredibly simple point; but it's hard to learn and remember. What we *want* to communicate is far less important than what the other person *understands*. And we can communicate without even meaning to, if someone pays attention to what we're doing (or not doing).

As Paul Watzlawick once said: we can't *not* communicate.

Let's return to that conversation we were having. Just as I can guess your meaning by interpreting the context of your answer, so you could think about the effect that your words and behaviour might be having on me. You could then adjust your behaviour so that I could understand you more easily. You might give me more details or do something to demonstrate what you want me to understand.

And, of course, at this point, you are also now paying attention to me. You're noticing my words and behaviour, making a best guess about what they might mean.

And so begins a subtle dance between us: a gentle exchange of attention. We start to mirror each other's stance and each other's gestures; our voices begin to chime together, matching rhythm, pace and pitch. We may even begin to anticipate each other's words and finish each other's sentences.

We're establishing rapport. Deep down, we begin to feel that we understand each other.

Building rapport

The images we use to describe rapport are not the images of railways or parcel couriers. We don't talk about transmitting information. Instead, we might use the language of music. You may feel that I'm 'on your wavelength'; I may feel that we're 'in tune'. Perhaps we feel 'a sense of harmony', or that 'we're singing from the same song sheet'.

We're using a different model of communication.

Most rapport occurs spontaneously. But we can also try to build rapport deliberately. And then rapport becomes more than a pleasurable behaviour. It becomes a communication skill.

To develop our rapport-building skills, we need to think about our:

- physical behaviour;
- vocal behaviour;
- verbal behaviour.

Overwhelmingly, we believe what we see. There is a famous sales phrase, 'the eye buys'. If there is a mismatch between what I say and what my body is doing, you are going to believe my body. So building rapport deliberately must begin with giving the physical signs of being welcoming, relaxed and open.

The music of the voice is the second key factor. We can vary our pitch (how high or low the tone of voice is), pace (the speed of speaking) and volume (how loudly or softly we speak). If you speak quickly and loudly, and raise the pitch of your voice, you will sound tense or stressed. And that tension will infect the other person, making them feel uneasy. If your vocal music is lower in tone, slower and softer, the other person will relax.

But creating rapport means more than matching body language or vocal tone. We must also match the other person's words, so that they feel we're 'speaking their language'.

For most of us, starting a conversation with someone we don't know is stressful. We can be lost for words. 'Breaking the ice' is a skill that many of us would dearly love to develop.

The key is to decrease the tension in the encounter. Look for something in your shared situation to talk about; then ask a question relating to that. The other person must not feel excluded or interrogated, so avoid:

- talking about yourself;
- asking the other person a direct question about themselves.

Doing either will increase the tension in the conversation. As will doing nothing! So take the initiative. Put them at ease, and you will soon relax yourself.

EXERCISE

Here is a simple method to establish rapport with someone you don't know. Try it out in the staff restaurant, at social gatherings, in networking meetings and at conferences:

1 Copy the other person's body language to create a 'mirror image'.

2 Ask three questions – but no more than three until you've done the next two things.

3 Find something from what you've just learned that will allow you to compliment the other person – subtly.

4 Find something in what you have found out to agree with.

5 Repeat steps 1–4 until the conversation takes on a life of its own.

(With thanks to Chris Dyas.)

A new definition of communication

We need a new definition of the word 'communication'. Attention, pattern matching, building rapport: we clearly need to replace the transmission model of communication with something more accurate. And the history of the word itself gives us a clue.

'Communication' derives from the Latin *communis*, meaning 'common', 'shared'. It belongs to the family of words that includes communion, communism and community. When we communicate, we are trying to share meaning.

Or, to put it another way:

> Communication is the process of creating shared understanding.

We seek to create shared understanding in all sorts of ways, using many different technologies. We speak on the phone and hold videoconferences; we make presentations and spend hours producing slides; we write e-mails and texts; we design web pages and publish blog posts.

But our basic mode of communication remains what it always has been: conversation. We hold conversations to build relationships and to make sense of reality. We influence each other's thoughts, feelings and actions by holding conversations. We converse to solve problems, to cooperate and find new things to do. Conversation is our way of imagining and creating the future.

Do you want to improve your communication skills? You could start by thinking about the conversations you hold. And that's what we'll do in the next chapter.

SUMMARY POINTS

- Communication begins not with transmission, but with understanding.
- Understanding is a pattern-matching process.
- Sometimes we have to fill in the gaps to make the pattern.
- The key to this skill is being able to read context.
- By asking 'What effect am I having?' in any conversation, we can begin to build rapport.
- We can build rapport deliberately, by managing our:
  - physical behaviour;
  - vocal behaviour;
  - verbal behaviour.
- Communication is the process of creating shared understanding.
- Conversation is the principal tool we use.

2 How conversations work

Conversations are verbal dances. The word 'conversation' derives from a Latin word meaning 'to move around with'.

Like any dance, conversations follow rules. The rules allow us to move in harmony, without stepping on each other's toes. Different kinds of conversation have different rules.

EXERCISE

Think about the words we use to describe different kinds of conversation. Write down a few of them. How do they differ? Can you identify any of the rules that apply to each?

For example, you might think of the word 'chat', and the word 'discussion'. What is the difference between the two? Do chats and discussions follow different rules?

Can you think of any other words describing kinds of conversation?

We hold so many conversations that the rules have become unconscious assumptions. As a result, if a conversation goes wrong, we may be baffled and have no idea how to put it right.

To begin with, let's bring a few of those assumptions to the surface.

The three basic rules of good conversation

These three rules make explicit some of our most basic assumptions about effective conversations:

- Rule one: one speaker at a time.
- Rule two: assume meaningful intent.
- Rule three: keep the conversation on TRAC.

Each of these three rules are discussed below.

Rule one: one speaker at a time

The first golden rule of good conversation is:

One speaker at a time.

The dance of conversation is made up of 'turns'. We take turns to speak and to listen.

One of the most important skills in conversation is knowing when to take your turn. If you start speaking during the other person's turn, they are likely to feel annoyed or insulted. If you want to avoid damaging your reputation, cultivate the skill of turn taking.

To take turns properly, we need to listen. Only by listening can we work out:

- when to take our turn;
- what to say.

We rarely think about it, but taking turns is a very subtle skill.

For a start, it is vitally important to *come in on cue* when you take your turn. If you leave too long a gap, the other person might start to worry. Research suggests that a gap of only half a second is long enough to attract the other person's attention and make them concerned or embarrassed.

Second, you need to *show that you've been listening*. If you don't do so, it will look as if you have not been paying attention; that you are not in the least interested in what the other person has been saying; that you are, in fact, a rather rude person.

And finally, when it is your turn to speak, *whatever you say has to be relevant* to what the other person has just said. If you say something completely unrelated to their last remarks, they will start to think that you're not just impolite and rude, but possibly crazy.

A lot rides on our ability to take turns. Get it right, and the conversation will go swimmingly. Get it wrong, and your long-term relationship might be in jeopardy. We need to learn this skill, and it takes time; if we're lucky, we learn it as children from our friends and families.

Here's how you follow the first rule of good conversation:

1 Prepare for the moment when the speaker finishes speaking.
2 Find something to say that demonstrates you have been listening to what they said.
3 Find a remark that links clearly and directly to their last turn.

Rule two: assume meaningful intent

The second golden rule of good conversation is:

Assume that the speaker wants to say something meaningful to you.

When we're listening in a conversation, we usually assume that the speaker is trying to say something that we will understand. Creating shared understanding: that's what communication is, right? And of course, the other person is usually assuming the same thing about us. We are both assuming, deep down, that we're cooperating: working together to generate shared meaning. Psychologists who study conversation call this assumption the 'cooperative principle'.

Of course, the cooperative principle sometimes breaks down (think of a conversation where you're talking at cross-purposes).

Sometimes we try deliberately to violate it (think of a heated argument, in which we might cry out: 'That's not what I mean!'). But, in general, we use the cooperative principle because it makes sense to do so. What is the point of paying attention if we're not trying to create shared understanding?

If you follow rule two, you will be ready to do two things:

- First, you will happily ignore any mistakes the speaker makes.
- Second, you will fill in the gaps between their words.

Most of us find it easy to do both. We usually ignore any mistakes that speakers make: errors of grammar or vocabulary, for example. We might not even notice those mistakes. Instead, we give the speaker the benefit of the doubt and focus on what they are trying to say.

We're also very good at filling in the gaps. Remember the Kanizsa triangle we looked at in Chapter 1? Just as we fill in the gaps of that image to make the triangle, so we fill in the gaps in conversations to create meaning.

Filling in the gaps might mean completing a speaker's statement or adding some details. If we *cannot* work out what the speaker means, we consider other possibilities. Perhaps they are deliberately lying or being obstructive; maybe they're drunk, mentally incapacitated or disturbed.

So, when we're listening, we ignore the speaker's mistakes and fill in the gaps. There is a good reason for making these two assumptions. After all, it will soon be our turn to speak. We will need to work out:

- *when* to speak; and
- *what* to say.

If we are using the cooperative principle, we will want the other person to understand us. We'll want our next turn to be as meaningful as possible. So we'll need to judge when the speaker has finished speaking and is ready to listen; and we'll have to find something to say that is more or less relevant to what they have just said.

To follow rule two of good conversation, follow these three steps:

1 Find the gaps in what the speaker is saying and try to fill them in.

2 If you are not sure what the speaker means, you might need to:
   - *complete* what they have said;
   - *clarify* something you do not quite understand; or
   - *convert* a statement in some way (because it is ironic, sarcastic, exaggerated, understated, metaphorical or expressed in jargon).

3 If necessary, use your next speaking turn in the conversation to check that you have understood what the other person has said. It is often a good idea to do this before making your next point.

Rule three: keep the conversation on TRAC

The third rule of effective conversation is:

Check for truth, relevance, adequacy and clarity.

The cooperative principle lays the foundation for four other assumptions we make in our conversations. When we're listening, we usually assume that the speaker will:

- speak the *truth* (they will not say what they know to be false; they have evidence for what they are saying);
- say something *relevant* to the purpose of the conversation;
- give us *adequate* information: as much as we need to understand, and no more;
- speak *clearly* (they will use words we know, avoid ambiguous words, speak only the number of words necessary, and put the words in a clear order).

These assumptions are based on the work of Paul Grice, a philosopher of language, who calls them 'conversational maxims'. We can remember these maxims by using a simple acronym:

True (the maxim of *quality*).

Relevant (the maxim of *relation*).

Adequate (the maxim of *quantity*).

Clear (the maxim of *manner*).

(In this list, the names in brackets are Grice's more formal names for these maxims.) And we can use these four maxims to keep our conversations, well, on TRAC.

FLOUTING THE MAXIMS

A speaker might violate one of the maxims without meaning to. When they do so, we might become confused; we might try to bring the conversation back on TRAC by drawing attention to the violation. But remember rule two: assume meaningful intent. If we think that the speaker is violating a maxim, we are much more likely to assume that they are doing so *deliberately*. Analysts call this *flouting* the maxim.

For example:

- If we think that a speaker's statement is *not true*, we might assume that they are deliberately lying.
- If they say something that seems *irrelevant* to us, we might assume that they are trying to change the subject.
- If what they say seems *inadequate*, we will often assume that they are deliberately holding something back.
- And if they use *unclear* words – words we don't understand – we might assume that they are trying to sound superior or make us look stupid.

Most of us can usually work out the hidden meaning behind the other person's remarks in a conversation. Sometimes, though, we find ourselves baffled. We cannot work out *why* a speaker's remarks are untrue, irrelevant, inadequate or unclear. Perhaps our previous remarks have been unclear? Perhaps they don't understand our language very well? Perhaps they are unwell...

USING THE MAXIMS TO IMPROVE OUR CONVERSATIONS

The maxims of conversation were not originally intended to be instructions. Grice saw them as the assumptions we usually make when we are talking to each other. But we can use his maxims as guidelines to improve our conversations.

If in doubt, we can check whether what we are saying – or hearing – is:

- *t*rue;
- *r*elevant;
- *a*dequate;
- *c*lear.

If you feel that the conversation is going wrong, try using one of the maxims to bring it back on TRAC.

The principal way to use the maxims as listeners is to ask questions; the principal way to use them as speakers is to make statements that refer to the maxims in some way.

EXERCISE

As a listener, what questions could you ask to bring a conversation back on TRAC?

I've suggested a couple of questions for each maxim. Can you think of any others?

True:

Are you sure that is correct?

What makes you say that?

▶

Relevant:

> I'm sorry, I cannot see how that links to what you have just said.
>
> What is the connection?

Adequate:

> Can you tell me more?
>
> What is the big idea here?

Clarity:

> Sorry, what does [*strange word*] mean?
>
> In other words... [*try to say what they have just said in your own words*].

Now, as a speaker, what statements could you make to help keep a conversation on TRAC?

Again, I've given you some ideas to start you thinking. Can you think of others?

True:

> I've got good evidence for this.
>
> Well, it is true in these circumstances...

Relevant:

> These things are connected.
>
> The point of all this is...

Adequate:

> Okay, I know – too much information!
>
> Maybe I need to tell you more.

Clarity:

> Maybe I'm talking jargon here.
>
> In other words... [*repeat what you have just said – in other words*].

Why do conversations go wrong?

If you follow the three basic rules given above, your conversations will immediately improve. They are 'quick hits'. With a little practice, we can all begin to:

- take our turn more effectively;
- focus on the meaning that the speaker is trying to convey;
- check remarks for truth, relevance, adequacy and clarity.

Now we can develop our skills further, by exploring the three dimensions of conversation:

- context;
- relationship;
- behaviour.

Putting conversations in context

Conversations always take place within a context. Many conversations fail because one or both of us ignore or misunderstand the context in which we are holding the conversation.

Part of that context will be the wider situation in which you are meeting. What is the reason for the conversation? Is it part of a larger conversation? If we don't check at the start *why* we are meeting, we may very quickly start to misunderstand each other.

Then there is the environmental context. Are you holding a conversation somewhere quiet, comfortable and private? Modern open-plan offices are often noisy, uncomfortable and all too public.

Finally, consider the conversation's cultural context. What are the norms in your organization about conversations? Are conversations valued where you work? Do some colleagues have a reputation for particularly good conversations? Or particularly bad ones? Do you have to go through any kind of routine or protocol

before you can hold a conversation (booking diary slots or rooms, for example)? Are some conversations valued more highly than others?

Other factors may make conversation difficult in your organization. It may lack social spaces – a staff restaurant, for example, or comfortable breakout spaces. People may be spread over different locations. More and more people are complaining that they hardly ever see their managers, let alone talk to them. (Are *you* one of those managers?)

If the conversation does happen, we might bring assumptions with us that can make the conversation more difficult. For example, we might assume that:

- we both know what we are talking about;
- we know how the other person views the situation;
- we shouldn't let our feelings show;
- the other person is somehow to blame for the problem;
- we can be brutally honest;
- we need to solve the other person's problem;
- we are right and they are wrong.

If we leave those assumptions unquestioned, then misunderstandings and conflict can quickly arise.

These assumptions derive from our mental patterns. (We encountered mental patterns in Chapter 1: the road sign, the Kanizsa triangle. We use mental patterns to make sense of incomplete or ambiguous information.) For example, I might have a mental pattern that we are in business to make a profit; that women have an inherently different management style from men; or that character is determined by some set of national characteristics.

All too often, conversations become conflicts between these mental patterns. This is *adversarial conversation*, and it is one of the most important and deadly reasons why conversations go wrong. (We will discuss adversarial conversation in Chapter 3.)

KEY QUESTIONS

Context

- Objectives: do you both know why you are holding the conversation?
- Time: is this the right time to be holding this conversation? What is the history behind the conversation? Is it part of a larger process?
- Place: are you conversing in a place that is comfortable, quiet and free from distractions?
- Assumptions: do you both understand the assumptions that you are starting from? Do you need to explore them before going further?

Working out the relationship

Our relationship defines how our conversations will go. We converse differently with complete strangers and with close acquaintances.

Human relationships operate in four dimensions:

- status;
- power;
- role;
- liking.

All of these factors define the territory of the conversation.

Status

Our status in any conversation is the rank we have in relation to the other person. Status is brutally simple: our status is either higher than the other person's, or lower.

Status is always relative and temporary. (We use *status symbols* – clothing, trophies, cars – precisely because our status in relation to others is always uncertain.) We gain our status from other people: it is evident in the way they behave towards us, the respect, familiarity or reserve they display with us. And, of course, we also influence other people's status by the way we behave towards them. And we do all this through conversation.

Status is like a seesaw. It works in only one dimension – up and down – and raising one end of the seesaw inevitably means lowering the other.

For example, we might want to *raise* our status. The seesaw of status, however, means that raising our status must mean lowering that of the other person. The shorthand for this kind of behaviour is 'pushing': examples of pushing, in increasing order of intensity, might include instructing, demanding, interrupting, criticizing or abusing.

Conversely, we might want to raise the other person's status. This kind of behaviour is often called 'pulling': examples of pulling, in increasing order of intensity, might include asking for their opinion, encouraging, praising, giving way, or agreeing with everything they say. Once again, raising the other person's status on the seesaw inevitably means lowering our own.

EXERCISE

What else could we say or do to 'push': to raise our status in a conversation? Note down some examples here.

What else could we say or do to 'pull' – to raise the other person's status? Note down some examples here.

Often, the most effective strategy in a conversation is to *equalize* status: to level the seesaw, as it were. Remember how we explored rapport in Chapter 1? Building rapport could be defined as the behaviour that levels our status relationship.

Power

Power is the control we can exert over others. If we can influence or control people's behaviour in any way, we have power over them. John French and Bertram Raven, in the late 1950s, identified five kinds of power:

- *reward power*: the ability to grant favours for behaviour;
- *coercive power*: the ability to punish others;
- *legitimate power*: conferred by law or other sets of rules;
- *referent power*: the 'charisma' that causes others to imitate or idolize;
- *expert power*: deriving from specific levels of knowledge or skill.

People are beginning to talk about a new form of power. *Convening power* is defined by the Foreign and Commonwealth Office as 'the ability to bring the right people together'. It is the power of 'connectors', who are often at the heart of effective networking. For more on this, see Chapter 9.

We might seek to exercise different kinds of power at different points in a conversation. If you have little reward power over the other person, for example, you might try to influence them as an expert. If you lack charisma or respect with the other person, you might try to exert authority by appealing to legitimate or to coercive power.

Role

A role is a set of behaviours that people expect of us. A formal role may be explicitly defined in a job description; an informal role is conferred on us as a result of people's experience of our conversations.

You might have taken part in exercises to find out your preferred role when working in teams. One of the most famous such exercises was developed by Meredith Belbin during the 1970s. 'A team is not a bunch of people with job titles', wrote Belbin, 'but a congregation of individuals, each of whom has a role that is understood by other members.'

Belbin's categories – he has nine, including team worker, co-ordinator, monitor-evaluator, shaper and so on – can help us to understand the way we hold conversations in teams and other work settings. But there is a danger that we can find ourselves labelled with the role identified in a questionnaire; worse, we might start labelling others with their Belbin role. As a result, our conversations can become limited by our mental models about those roles.

Liking

Conversations can fail because we dislike each other. But they can also go wrong because we like each other a lot!

Liking and disliking can be more complicated than the simple terms suggest. Liking can become an emotional entanglement or even a fully-fledged relationship; dislike can turn a conversation into a long-term vendetta.

Territory

The above four factors – status, power, role and liking – define the *territory* of a conversation.

A successful conversation seeks out shared territory: the common ground between us. But we guard our own territory carefully. As a result, many conversational rules are about asking and giving permission to enter each other's territory.

KEY QUESTIONS

Relationship

- Status: is there a marked difference in status between you? Why is that? How does this difference affect the way you are behaving towards the other person? How do you think it might be affecting their behaviour?

- Power: can you see power being wielded in the conversation? What kind of power? In which direction? How might you both be affecting the power relationship? How do you want to affect it?

- Role: what is your role in this conversation? Think about your formal role (your job title, perhaps, or contractual position) and your informal role. How do people see you acting in conversations? Can you feel yourself falling naturally into any particular role in the conversation?

- Liking: how is the conversation being affected by your feelings towards each other? Is the liking or disliking getting in the way of a productive outcome?

- Territory: where are the boundaries? Are you finding common ground? Where can you give permission for the other person to enter your territory? Where can you ask permission to enter theirs?

Managing behaviour

Conversations are never simply exchanges of words. We also use *non-verbal communication*: the music of our voice, our gestures, the way we move our eyes or hold our body, the physical positions we adopt in relation to each other. 'Under pressure', writes Tracy Cox, 'our bodies leak. Our true feelings come gushing out in gestures.'

Non-verbal behaviour is largely unconscious. Actors (and con artists) can control their non-verbal behaviour consciously, but it takes a lot of training. Most of us learn body language simply by absorbing and imitating the body language of people around us. As a result, our non-verbal communication will sometimes say things to the other person that we don't intend them to know. (Remember that key question in Chapter 1? *What effect am I having?*)

Conversations often go wrong because we misinterpret non-verbal messages. There are four main reasons for this:

- *Non-verbal messages are ambiguous.* No dictionary can accurately define them. Their meaning can vary according to context. Some people close their eyes in order to concentrate on what you are saying; others do so to try to avoid paying you attention.

- *Non-verbal messages are continuous.* We can stop talking but we cannot stop behaving!

- *Non-verbal messages are multichannel.* Everything happens at once: eyes, hands, feet, body position. We interpret non-verbal messages holistically, as a whole impression. This makes them strong but unspecific: we may not be able to pin down what the behaviour is suggesting to us.

- *Non-verbal messages are culturally determined.* Research suggests that a few non-verbal messages are universal: everyone seems to smile when they are happy, for example. Most non-verbal behaviours, however, are specific to a culture. A lot of confusion can arise from the misinterpretation of non-verbal messages across a cultural divide.

Effective communicators manage their behaviour. They work hard to align their non-verbal messages with their words. You may feel that trying to manage your behaviour is dishonest: 'play-acting' a part that you don't feel. But we all act a little when we hold conversations. Managing our behaviour simply means trying to act appropriately: trying to have the right effect on the other person.

If you want to work on your non-verbal communication, start with your eyes. If you think more about where you are looking during a conversation, you can find ways to give your words added weight. At its simplest, by looking steadily at the other person and keeping fairly still, you will probably immediately make the conversation more comfortable.

KEY QUESTIONS

Managing behaviour

- *Look for clusters.* If you are picking up a group of non-verbal messages that seem to indicate a single feeling, you may be able to trust your interpretation more fully.

- *Consider past experience.* We can interpret more accurately the behaviour of people we know. We certainly notice *changes* in their behaviour. We also interpret patterns of behaviour over time more accurately than single instances.

- *Check your perceptions.* Ask questions. You are interpreting observed behaviour, not reading someone's mind. Check out what you observe and make sure that your interpretation is accurate.

- *Work on your eyes and your gestures.* Think about where you are looking during the conversation and how you are moving.

The uses of conversation

Conversation is what human beings do. We use conversations to establish and maintain relationships with each other, to share useful information and to inspire each other to act. This subtle dance of speaking and listening is an essential life skill.

All the other modes of communication that we explore in this book are related, in some way, to conversation. In Chapter 4, we look at the skills of enquiry, which build on our powers of listening. Chapter 5 looks at the complementary skills of persuasion: how we influence each other's thoughts and feelings by speaking.

Chapter 6 explores tough conversations: the conversations we might want to avoid, or that suddenly erupt when we least expect them. Chapters 7 and 8 discuss what we might call 'conversation at a distance'. A presentation, for example, is a conversation in which taking turns is strictly restricted. And writing is a kind of conversation that lacks most aspects of non-verbal communication, and in which context can all too often be forgotten. And yet the new technologies – e-mail, texting, instant messaging, Twitter – are part of a wider trend to bring writing closer to the spoken word, a trend that brings new challenges and the need for new skills.

Finally, in Chapter 9, we look at networking. Increasingly, we need to be able to communicate with strangers – quickly, comfortably and productively. Networking is a new kind of conversation, and it holds the key to success in many areas of our lives.

But first, let's look a little more at conversation: this most powerful and fascinating of communication skills. How can we improve the conversations we hold – at home, at work and in social situations? Chapter 3 provides some suggestions.

SUMMARY POINTS

- The three basic rules of good conversation:
  - Only one speaker should speak at a time.
  - Assume that the speaker wants to say something meaningful to you.
  - Keep the conversation on TRAC. As a listener and a speaker, check for: truth; relevance; adequacy; clarity.
- Use questions when listening, and statements when speaking.
- To improve the *context* of your conversations, check that:
  - the objectives are clear;
  - the time and place are right;
  - you are both making the same assumptions to start with.
- To improve the *relationship* in your conversations, manage:
  - the status relationship between you;
  - the power dynamics in the conversation;
  - the roles you are taking in the conversation;
  - your personal feelings about each other;
  - whether or not you are comfortably on common ground.
- And to improve the *non-verbal behaviour* in the conversation:
  - look for clusters;
  - consider past experience;
  - check your perceptions;
  - work on your eyes and gestures.

3 Seven ways to improve your conversations

We hold all sorts of conversations at work. Some are relaxed chats (often called 'water-cooler talk'); others are planned. How can we make them more productive?

In this chapter, we look at seven proven strategies:

- Clarify your objective.
- Structure your thinking.
- Manage your time.
- Find common ground.
- Move beyond argument.
- Summarize often.
- Use visuals.

Don't feel that you must apply all seven at once. Take a single strategy and work at it for a few days. (You should have plenty of conversations to practise on!) Once you feel that you have integrated one skill into your conversations, move on to another.

Clarify your objective

Think of a conversation as a journey you are taking with another person. It will very quickly start to wander off track if you don't know where you're going. You will reach your destination only if you know where you're aiming for.

State your objective clearly at the start. We call this technique 'headlining': newspapers use headlines to give the reader the key message of a story, and we can do something similar in our conversations:

I want to talk to you about the development plan.

I know you're worried about the sales figures. I've got some clues that might help.

I've called this meeting to make a decision about project X.

Of course, you might decide to change your objective in the middle of the conversation – just as you might decide to change direction in the middle of a journey. That's fine, as long as everyone in the conversation knows what is going on. Indeed, if you make your objective too specific at the start of the conversation, you might limit your options for success at the end. In a negotiation, for example, think about different possible destinations: what is your preferred outcome, what would you be willing to settle for, and what is non-negotiable?

Objectives roughly divide into two categories: 1) exploring a problem; 2) finding a solution. When you're thinking about your headline, ask: 'problem or solution?' We often assume that any conversation about a problem is aiming to find a solution. As a result, we may find ourselves working towards a solution without accurately defining or understanding the problem. (More on this in the next section, 'Structure your thinking'.)

In a meeting, the best place to announce the objectives of the conversation is on the agenda. That word means 'things to be done'.

Use your agenda to list what you want to *do* in the meeting, not just what you want to talk about. For example, rather than a bald heading such as 'IT infrastructure', write something like 'Review supplier options for IT support and choose preferred bidder'. You have stated the conversation's objective; now everyone in the meeting knows where the conversation should be going.

Structure your thinking

You can improve your conversations enormously by giving them structure. The simplest way to structure a conversation is to break it in half.

We can imagine thinking as a process in two stages. We do *first-stage thinking* when we are working out what we're thinking about; we do *second-stage thinking* when we are working out what to do about it. First-stage thinking explores reality and translates what we have found into language; second-stage thinking then manipulates the language to decide on an action. We could say that first-stage thinking is perception, and second-stage thinking is judgement.

We often ignore first-stage thinking. We may assume that we know what we are looking at. But, of course, the quality of our second-stage thinking depends directly on the quality of our first-stage thinking. If our perception of a situation is limited, then our judgement about it will be limited. If we misunderstand a problem, then we may come up with a poor solution.

I sometimes think that we are obsessed with solutions. Under pressure of time and the drive for results, we often leap to second-stage thinking without spending nearly enough time in the first stage. We may not *want* to look at a problem too hard; after all, problems can be frightening, and living with an unresolved problem can be uncomfortable. Better to deal with it: sort it out, solve it, get rid of it.

Try to avoid leaping to second-stage thinking. Give the first stage – the problem stage – as much attention and time as you can. Then give it a little more. And make sure that all participants in the conversation are at the same stage of thinking at the same time.

The trick is to find the link between the two stages of thinking. Skilled conversationalists work on linking:

- the past and the present;
- the problem and the solution;
- requests and answers;
- negative ideas and positive ideas;
- opinions about what is true with speculation about the consequences.

Four types of conversation

We can break down the two stages of thinking into four conversations. These are conversations for:

- relationship;
- possibility;
- opportunity;
- action.

These four conversations may form part of a single, larger conversation; they may also take place separately, at different stages of a process or project (see Figure 3.1).

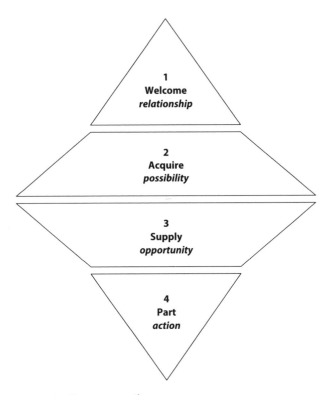

FIGURE 3.1 Four conversations

A CONVERSATION FOR RELATIONSHIP

This is an exploratory conversation. We hold this conversation to create or develop the relationship we need in order to achieve our objective.

Key questions in this conversation will include:

- *Who are we?*
- *What is the problem?*
- *How do you define the problem?*
- *How do we relate to the matter in hand?*

- *What links us?*
- *How do we see things?*
- *What do you see that I cannot see?*
- *What do I see that you do not see?*
- *In what ways do we see things similarly, or differently?*

Conversations for relationship may be tentative, awkward or embarrassing. We often rush them. Think of those tricky conversations we hold with strangers at parties. A good conversation for relationship moves beyond the 'What do you do? Where do you live?' questions. We are defining our relationship to each other, and to the matter in hand.

A CONVERSATION FOR POSSIBILITY

A conversation for possibility continues the exploration: it develops first-stage thinking. It asks what we *might* be looking at.

Key questions in a conversation for possibility include:

- *What is the* real *problem?*
- *What are we really trying to do?*
- *Is this a problem?*
- *How could we look at this from a different angle?*
- *Can we interpret this differently?*
- *How could we do this?*
- *What does it look like from another person's point of view?*
- *What makes this different from last time?*
- *Have we ever done anything like this before?*
- *Can we make this simpler?*
- *Can we look at this in bits?*
- *What is this like?*
- *What does this feel or look like?*

A conversation for possibility is *not* about whether to do something, or what to do. It seeks to find new ways of looking at the problem.

We could find all sorts of new ways of looking at a problem:

- Look at it from a new angle.
- Ask for different interpretations of what is happening.
- Try to distinguish what you are looking at from what you think about it.
- Ask how other people might see it.
- Break the problem into parts.
- Isolate one part of the problem and look at it in detail.
- Connect the problem into a wider network of ideas.
- Ask what the problem is like. What does it look like, or feel like?

Conversations for possibility can be very creative: brainstorming is a good example. But exploring different points of view can also create conflict: what Edward de Bono calls 'adversarial thinking'. (More about adversarial thinking shortly and in Chapter 6.)

This isn't decision time. If you are chairing a meeting, for example, encourage people to give you ideas, and take care not to judge or criticize them – either the ideas or the person. Manage the emotional content of this conversation with particular care. Ask, gently, for the evidence to support expressions of feeling.

A CONVERSATION FOR OPPORTUNITY

A conversation for opportunity takes us into second-stage thinking.

Key questions in this conversation include:

- *Where can we act?*
- *What could we do?*
- *Which possibilities do we build on?*
- *Which possibilities are feasible?*

- *What target do we set ourselves?*
- *Where are the potential obstacles?*
- *How will we know that we have succeeded?*

This conversation focuses on future action: in choosing from among a number of possibilities, you are finding a sense of common purpose. So this conversation is about planning. Many of our good ideas never become reality because we don't map out paths of opportunity. A conversation for opportunity constructs such a path. Assess what you would need to make action possible: resources, support and skills.

The bridge from possibility to opportunity is *measurement*. Begin to set targets, milestones, obstacles, measures of success. How will you be able to judge when you have achieved an objective?

Backward planning can often be more effective than forward planning. Recall your original objective. Has it changed? Place yourselves in a future where you have achieved your objective. What does such a future look like and feel like? What is happening? What do you need to do to create that future? Backward planning may allow you to simplify the plan and find new opportunities for action.

A CONVERSATION FOR ACTION

In this conversation, you agree what to do, who will do it and when it will happen. Translating opportunity into action needs more than agreement; you need to generate a promise, a *commitment* to act.

A conversation for action is absolutely essential at the end of an interview or meeting. After all, if nothing happens as a result of these conversations, why hold them? A conversation for action balances asking and promising. If necessary, take this conversation step by step.

HOW TO HOLD A CONVERSATION FOR ACTION

1 Ask the other person to do something by a certain time. Make it clear that this is a request, not an order. Orders may get immediate results, but they rarely generate commitment.

2 The other person now has four possible answers to this request:
- They can accept.
- They can decline.
- They may commit to accepting or declining at a later date. ('*I'll let you know by...*')
- They can make a counter-offer. ('*I can't do that, but I can do...*')

3 Negotiate until the other person is able to make a firm promise. '*I will do x for you by time y.*'

The person making the promise should use this precise wording. Don't settle for a simple 'Yes, I'll do that.' If they *specify* what they will do, and by when – and if they themselves write that action down – then they are more likely to do it. Use this technique to gain commitment to actions at the end of a meeting. If people promise to do something, publicly, and write it down, they are more likely to do what they promise.)

These four conversations will only be truly effective if you hold them *in order*. The success of each conversation depends on the success of the conversation before it. If you fail to resolve a conversation, it will continue underneath the next *in code*. Unresolved aspects of a conversation for relationship, for instance, can become conflicts of possibility, hidden agendas or 'personality clashes'.

Possibilities left unexplored become lost opportunities. And promises to act that have no real commitment behind them may mean that things do not get done.

Manage your time

Conversations take time, and time is the one entirely non-renewable resource. Manage time well, both for and in your conversations.

Managing time for the conversation

Work out how much time you have. Don't just assume that there is *no* time. Be realistic. If necessary, make an appointment to hold the interview later, or schedule the meeting for another time.

Managing time in the conversation

Most conversations speed up and slow down at different times. Generally, an effective conversation will probably start quite slowly and get faster as it goes on. But there are no real rules about this.

Conversations can go too fast for all sorts of reasons. Paradoxically, agreement and conflict can both cause conversations to speed up. You may have settled on a solution too quickly or have succumbed to 'groupthink' (in which everyone thinks alike because it feels comforting). Alternatively, a disagreement may have flared into an emotional argument.

Conversely, conversations can become painfully slow when we find ourselves stuck with a problem (or with only one view of a problem). If you hear people analysing the past instead of looking to the future, or people wandering off the subject, it is likely that you need to inject the conversation with new energy.

Of course, it is all very well being able to see if a conversation is going too fast or too slow – but how can we regain control of its pace?

EXERCISE

Spend a morning monitoring the pace of your conversations. Which ones went too fast? Which were too slow? During the afternoon, continue monitoring but take action to adjust the pace of the conversation. If the conversation is going too slowly, close down sections of the conversation by summarizing; push for action or move from remarks to implications: 'what does this mean in terms of...?' If the conversation is going too fast, slow it down by reflecting or paraphrasing before responding, by asking open questions (questions beginning with one of the 'w' words – 'why?' is a good candidate) or by simply pausing.

Find common ground

The most satisfying conversations create the sense that we have found common ground. We may have each started in our own territory, with our own points of view; by the end of the conversation, we have found the place where we can stand together, facing the future. To find that place, we may need to move: to change our position, to shift our point of view. Conversation – moving around together – is the means by which we achieve that.

We ask for, and give, permission for these moves to happen. If you are asking permission to move into new territory, you might:

- make a remark tentatively;
- express yourself hesitantly ('Perhaps we might...' 'I suppose I think...' 'It's possible that...');
- pause before speaking;
- look away or look down a lot;

- explicitly ask permission ('Do you mind if I mention...' 'May I speak freely about...');
- make a tentative remark about the other person's words or behaviour.

Don't proceed until the other person has given their permission. They might do so explicitly ('Please say what you like'; 'I would really welcome your honest opinion'; 'I don't mind you talking about that'). Or they might give permission without using words: nodding, smiling, leaning forward.

Conversely, refusing permission can be explicit – 'I'd rather we didn't talk about this' – or in code. The person may evade your question, answer vaguely or reply with another question. Their non-verbal behaviour may hint at their real feelings: folding their arms, sitting back in the chair, becoming restless, evading eye contact.

Move beyond argument

Ask anyone what they think of something, and the chances are they will tell you what is wrong with it. Too often, we assume that arguing for or against an idea is the only way to explore it. Adversarial thinking seems to be deeply engrained in us, perhaps because so many of us learn the skills of debating at school.

A debate is like a verbal boxing match. (The word derives from Latin, 'to beat down'). By the rules of debate, your opinions are somehow proved to be correct if you can successfully discredit any opposing opinions. You don't even have to prove that an idea is wrong; merely by ridiculing or discrediting the person voicing it, you may be able to persuade others that you are right. (This is often called an *ad hominem* argument.)

But argument – however formally conducted – *stops* us exploring and discovering new ideas. And argument can threaten the quality of the conversation itself by raising its emotional temperature:

people can become too busy defending themselves, too frightened, too battle fatigued, to do any better.

The ladder of inference

The 'ladder of inference' (Figure 3.2) takes our conversations beyond argument. The model was developed initially by Chris Argyris, who pictures the way we think in conversations as a ladder. At the bottom of the ladder is observation; at the top, action:

- From our observation, we step onto the first rung of the ladder by selecting *data*. (We choose what to look at.)
- On the second rung, we infer *meaning* from our experience of similar data.
- On the third rung, we generalize those meanings into *assumptions*.
- On the fourth rung, we construct mental models (or *beliefs*) out of those assumptions.
- We act on the basis of our mental models.

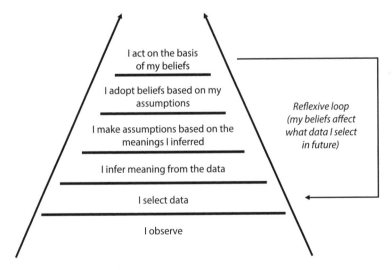

FIGURE 3.2 The ladder of inference

We travel up and down this ladder whenever we hold a conversation. We are often much better at climbing up than stepping down; in fact, we can leap up all the rungs in a few seconds. These 'leaps of abstraction' allow us to act more quickly but they can also limit the scope of the conversation. Even more worryingly, our mental models help us to leap back down the ladder and select data from future observation – thus limiting the range of the conversation still further. Argyris calls this a 'reflexive loop'; you might call it a mindset.

The ladder of inference gives us more choices about where to go in a conversation. It *slows down* our thinking. It allows us to:

- become more aware of our own thinking;
- make that thinking available to others;
- ask others about their thinking.

Above all, we can defuse an adversarial conversation by 'climbing down' from private beliefs, assumptions and opinions and then 'climbing up' to shared meanings and beliefs.

The key to using the ladder of inference is to ask questions:

- *What is the data that underlies what you have said?*
- *Do we agree on the data?*
- *Do we agree on what they mean?*
- *Can you take me through your reasoning?*
- *When you say [what you have said], do you mean [my rewording of it]?*

For example, if one of us suggests a course of action, the other can carefully climb down the ladder by asking:

- *'Why do you think this might work?' 'What makes this a good plan?'*
- *'What assumptions do you think you might be making?' 'Have you considered...?'*

- *'How would this affect...?' 'Does this mean that...?'*
- *'Can you give me an example?' 'What led you to look at this in particular?'*

Even more powerfully, the ladder of inference can help us to offer our own thinking for the other person to examine. If we are suggesting a plan of action, we can ask them:

- *'Can you see any flaws in my thinking?'*
- *'Would you look at this stuff differently?' 'How would you put this together?'*
- *'Would this look different in different circumstances?' 'Are my assumptions valid?'*
- *'Have I missed anything?'*

The beauty of this model is that you do not need any special training to use it. You can use it immediately, as a practical way to intervene in conversations that are descending into argument.

EXERCISE

Draw a picture of the ladder of inference on a piece of paper and add some of the questions listed above, near different rungs of the ladder. Put the paper in your wallet or bag – somewhere you can find it easily. Next time you find yourself disagreeing with someone in a conversation, take out the paper and use it to try, deliberately, to climb up or down the ladder. Ask questions; test assumptions; show the links in your own thinking; and ask the other person to show the links in theirs. See where the conversation goes. Then reflect on how useful the ladder of inference was as a conversation tool.

Summarize often

Summaries help us to do everything else we have been discussing in this chapter. They allow us to state our objective and check that we both share the same one. They allow us to structure the conversation and check where we are in our journey through first- and second-stage thinking. They help us to manage time and seek common ground; and they can help us to defuse argument.

Summarizing is not merely repeating what the other person has just said. To summarize means to reinterpret their ideas in your own language. It involves:

- *recognizing* the specific point they have made;
- *appreciating* the position from which they say it;
- *understanding* the beliefs that inform that position.

Recognizing what someone says does not imply that you agree with it. It *does* imply that you are thinking about what they have said. Appreciating their feelings does not mean you feel the same way, but it *does* show that you recognize those feelings. And understanding what they believe may not mean that you share their belief; but it *does* mean that you respect it. All of which means that summaries can contribute to shared problem solving.

Use visuals

Many of our conversations use visual elements. Look around at people chatting in restaurants and bars, at the way their hand gestures and facial expressions enrich the meaning of their words. And there are lots of other ways in which we can make our thinking visible. We could scribble on a bit of paper, draw on a flipchart or create a slide presentation. We could build a model or show someone how something works. Some of the most powerful visuals are the images we create in our listeners' minds with the words we use.

Recording your ideas on paper

Conversations – especially group conversations such as meetings – nearly always benefit from being recorded visually. The patterns and pictures and doodles that we scribble on a pad help us to listen, to summarize and to keep track of what we have covered. They can also become the *focus* for the conversation: when everyone can see what we are thinking about, we can think more efficiently and effectively.

Mind maps are a powerful way to visualize our thinking. In particular, they help us to do first-stage thinking – linking elements and encouraging us to find new ways of looking at something. Mind maps can not only record our thinking, but also improve it.

EXERCISE

Use this exercise next time you need to organize your thoughts about a project, a report or a presentation:

1 Put a visual image of your subject at the centre of a plain piece of paper.

2 Write down anything that comes to mind that connects to the central idea. Don't edit or block any ideas; every idea has the potential to be useful.

3 Write single words, in BLOCK CAPITALS, along lines radiating from the centre.

   Main ideas will tend to gravitate to the centre of the map; details will radiate towards the edge.

   Every line must connect to at least one other line.

   Use visual display: colour, pattern, highlights.

   Identify the groups of ideas that you have created. If you wish, give each a heading and put the groups into a number order.

Try out mind maps – in relatively simple conversations to begin with. Record a phone conversation using a mind map and see how well you get on with the technique. Extend your practice to face-to-face conversations and invite the other person to look at and contribute to the map. Mind maps can be powerful aids in meetings, when the dynamics of conversation become more complicated. Many managers use them to record meetings, and as the notes for minute writing.

Using metaphors

Metaphors are images of ideas in concrete form. The word means 'transferring' or 'carrying over': a metaphor carries your meaning from one thing to another. It enables your listener to *see* something in a new way, by picturing it as something else. Metaphor uses the imagination to support and develop your ideas.

We use many metaphors without even noticing them. If you want to extend your use of metaphors, start by listening out for them in your everyday conversations.

EXERCISE

Here is a useful exercise to open up your thinking about a problem. It is especially helpful if you are completely stuck and cannot find any solution:

1 Start by writing down the problem. You could define the problem either as a statement of what is wrong, or as a 'how to'.

For example, the problem might be either 'the team isn't working well together' or 'how to help the team work better together'.

2 Now ask yourself these questions:
- What is the problem like?
- If this were a different situation – a game of cricket, a medieval castle, a mission to Mars, a kindergarten – how would we deal with it?
- How would a different kind of person manage the issue: a gardener, a politician, an engineer, a hairdresser, an actor?
- What does this situation *feel* like?
- If this problem were an animal, what species of animal would it be?
- Describe the problem as if it were part of the human body.

3 Now try to find connections from the metaphors you have discovered back to the original problem. What does a metaphor suggest about future actions?

You probably need to slow down the conversation to find these metaphors. You will know when you have found a productive metaphor. ('Found' in that sentence is a metaphor.) The conversation will suddenly catch fire (that's another metaphor!). You will feel a sudden injection of energy (and there's a third metaphor) as you realize that you are looking at the issue in a completely new way.

SUMMARY POINTS

- There are seven proven strategies to help you to improve your conversations:
  - clarify your objective;
  - structure your thinking;
  - manage your time;
  - find common ground;
  - move beyond argument;
  - summarize often;
  - use visuals.
- To clarify your objective:
  - state your objective clearly at the start;
  - ask: problem or solution?
- To structure your thinking:
  - use first-stage thinking and second-stage thinking;
  - hold conversations for: relationship, possibility, opportunity, action.
- To manage your time:
  - manage time *for* the conversation;
  - manage time *in* the conversation.
- To find common ground:
  - ask for permission to move onto the other person's territory;
  - give permission for the other person to move onto your territory.
- To move beyond argument:
  - use the ladder of inference to check the other person's thinking;

- – use the ladder of inference to invite the other person to check your thinking.
- Summarize:
  - – at the start of the conversation;
  - – regularly throughout the conversation;
  - – at the end of the conversation.
- Use visuals:
  - – record your ideas;
  - – use mind maps;
  - – use metaphors.

4 The skills of enquiry

The skills of enquiry are the skills of listening. And the quality of your conversation depends on the quality of your listening.

Stephen Covey famously said: 'Seek first to understand, then to be understood.' Only by enquiring into the other person's ideas can you respond honestly and fully to them. Only by finding out how they think can you begin to persuade them to your way of thinking.

But skilled enquiry also helps the speaker. Listening – real, deep, attentive listening – can actually help them to think better.

I've summarized the skills of enquiry under seven headings:

- paying attention;
- treating the speaker as an equal;
- cultivating ease;
- encouraging;
- asking quality questions;
- rationing information;
- giving positive feedback.

Acquiring these skills will help you to give the other person the respect and space they deserve in order to develop their own ideas – to make their thinking visible.

Paying attention

Paying attention is one of the most respectful things we can do with another person. Paying attention means concentrating on what they are saying. That sounds simple: how can we listen without paying attention?

Of course, we often do just that. Nancy Kline puts it well, in her book, *Time to Think*:

> *We think we listen, but we don't. We finish each other's sentences, we interrupt each other, we moan together, we fill in the pauses with our own stories, we look at our watches, we sigh, frown, tap our finger, read the newspaper, or walk away. We give advice, give advice, give advice.*

Real listening means pausing our own thinking and allowing the speaker's thinking to enter our mind.

Paying attention helps a speaker to find their ideas and express them. If we are paying proper attention, the speaker will become more articulate. And if we are not paying attention, they will stumble and hesitate. Poor attention makes them more stupid; close attention makes them more intelligent.

Don't rush. Adjust your own tempo to that of the other person. Wait longer than you want to. And when they cannot think of anything else to say, ask: 'What else do you think about this? What else can you think of? What else comes to mind?' That invitation to talk more can bring even the weariest brain back to life.

Interrupting

Interrupting is the most obvious symptom of poor attention. Sometimes, we can't resist it. Some demon inside us seems to compel us to fill the speaker's pauses with words. It's as if the very idea of silence terrifies us.

Mostly, we interrupt because we are making assumptions. Next time you interrupt someone in a conversation, ask yourself which of these assumptions you are applying:

- My idea is better than theirs.
- The answer is more important than the problem.
- I have to utter my idea fast and if I don't interrupt, I'll lose my chance (or forget it).
- I know what they are going to say.
- They don't need to finish the sentence because my rewrite is an improvement.
- They can't improve this idea any further, so I might as well improve it for them.
- I'm more important than they are.
- It is more important for me to be seen to have a good idea than for me to let them finish.
- Interrupting will save time.

If you are assuming you know what the speaker is about to say, you are probably wrong. If you allow them to continue, they will often come up with something more interesting, more vivid and more personal than what you assumed.

EXERCISE

Next time you hold a conversation with a colleague, deliberately note down the number of times you interrupt them – and the number of times they interrupt you. When the conversation has finished, count up the two totals. What do the numbers suggest? How many of those interruptions were useful or necessary? (Not every interruption is unhelpful.)

Allowing quiet

Once you stop interrupting, the conversation will become quieter. Pauses will appear. The other person will stop talking and you will not fill the silence.

Think of these pauses as junctions in the journey of your conversation. You have a number of choices about where you might go next. Either of you might choose. If you want to switch from listening to persuading, you might make the choice. But, if you are enquiring, then you give the speaker the privilege of making the choice.

There are two kinds of pause. One is a filled pause; the other is empty. Learn to distinguish between the two.

Some pauses are filled with thought. Sometimes, the speaker will stop, perhaps suddenly. They will look elsewhere, probably into a longer distance. They are busy on an excursion – you are not invited. But they will want you to be there at the junction when they come back. You're privileged that they have trusted you to wait. So wait.

The other kind of pause is an empty one. Nothing much is happening. The speaker does not stop suddenly; instead, they seem to fade away. You are standing at the junction in the conversation together, and neither of you is moving. The energy seems to drop out of the conversation. The speaker's eyes don't focus anywhere. If they are comfortable in your company, they may focus on you as a cue for you to choose what move to make.

Wait out the pause. If the pause is empty, the speaker will probably say so in a few moments. 'I can't think of anything else.' 'That's it, really.' 'So. There we are. I'm stuck now.' Try asking: 'Can you think of anything else?' If the other person is ready for you to take the lead, then do so: ask a question, make a suggestion.

Showing that you are paying attention

The best way to look as if you are paying attention is – well, to pay attention. But sometimes we need to consciously work at paying attention. Begin with your eyes: practise looking steadily at the speaker when you are listening to them, and start to notice when you glance away. Generally, we don't look nearly enough at the people we are listening to.

Working on our eye movements benefits both listener and speaker. If you look more attentively, you will actually pay more attention to what the speaker is saying. (The speaker will probably look away from you more frequently; it is what we do when we are thinking about what to say.) Relax your facial muscles: no frowns or rigid smiles. Use minimal encouragers (more about those in the section on 'encouraging' below.) But come back, always, to the way you use your eyes.

Be aware that such attentive looking may actually inhibit the speaker. In some cultures, looking equates to staring and signals disrespect. You need to be sensitive to these possible individual or cultural distinctions and adapt your eye movements accordingly.

Treating the speaker as an equal

You will only enquire well if you treat the speaker as an equal. If you place yourself higher than them in status, you will discourage them from thinking well. If you place them higher than you, your own inhibitions may interfere with your attention.

Patronizing the speaker is the greatest enemy of equality in conversations. This conversational sin derives from the way we are treated as children – and the way some people subsequently treat children. Sometimes children have to be treated like children. We need to:

- decide for them;
- direct them;
- tell them what to do;
- assume that adults know better than they do;
- worry about them;
- take care of them;
- control them;
- think for them.

Sometimes, we carry this patronizing behaviour over into conversations with other adults. As soon as you think you know better than the other person, or provide the answers for them, or suggest that their thinking is inadequate, you are patronizing them. You cannot patronize someone and pay them close attention at the same time.

Treat the other person as an equal and you won't be able to patronize them.

Cultivating ease

Good thinking happens in a relaxed environment. Cultivating ease will allow you to enquire more deeply, and discover more ideas. When you are at ease, the solution to a problem will sometimes appear as if by magic.

Many people are uncomfortable with the idea of ease in the workplace. They are so used to urgency that they cannot imagine working in any other way. Many organizations equate ease with sloth. If you're not working flat out in these enterprises, chasing deadlines and juggling 50 assignments at the same time, you're not worth your salary. It is sometimes assumed that the best thinking happens in such a climate.

Not so. Urgency keeps people from thinking well; they are too busy *doing*. After all, doing is what gets results, isn't it? Well, not when people have to think to get those results. Sometimes, the best results only appear by *not* doing: by paying attention to someone else's ideas with a mind that is alert, comfortable and at ease.

Cultivating ease is largely a behavioural skill. You do not have to *feel* at ease to promote ease in another person. (How would you speak to a person who is threatening you with a gun, for example?) Breathe out, slow down your speaking rhythm, lower the volume and the pitch of your voice. Banish distractions: unplug the phone, close the door, find somewhere quiet and comfortable. (You may need to leave the office.) Make time. If the time is not right, postpone the conversation until ease is easier to achieve.

Encouraging

In order to liberate the other person's ideas, you may need to do more than pay attention, treat them as an equal and cultivate ease. You may need to actively encourage them to give you their ideas.

We're back with that key question we discovered in Chapter 1: *What effect am I having?* The speaker's thinking is largely the result of the effect you are having on them. So if you:

- suggest that they change the subject;
- try to convince them of your point of view before listening to their point of view;
- reply tit-for-tat to their remarks; or
- encourage them to compete with you,

you are not encouraging them to develop their thinking. You're not enquiring properly.

One of the worst enemies of encouragement is competitiveness. We can so easily find ourselves using the speaker's ideas to promote our own. It's all part of that habit of adversarial thinking.

Competition forces people to think only those thoughts that will help them win. If the speaker feels that you are competing with them, they will limit not only what they say but also what they think. Conversely, if you feel that the speaker is trying to compete with you, do not allow yourself to enter the competition. The ladder of inference (see Chapter 3) is one very powerful tool that will help you to defuse competitiveness in your conversations.

Instead of competing, welcome the difference in your points of view. Then try to find common ground. (Look back at Chapter 3.)

MINIMAL ENCOURAGERS

Minimal encouragers are brief, supportive actions that show the speaker that you want them to continue. They can be:

- sub-vocalizations: 'uh-huh', 'mm';
- words and phrases: 'right', 'really?', 'I see';
- repeated key words.

Behaviours can include:

- leaning forward;
- focusing eye contact;
- head nodding.

Minimal encouragers support the speaker without interrupting them. They demonstrate your interest, both generally and in particular points that the speaker is making. But beware: they could subtly influence the speaker to say what they think you want to hear, rather than what they want to say. And, poorly used, they can signal impatience or become an empty gesture.

Asking quality questions

Questions are at the heart of enquiry. That's obvious: enquiring *is* asking a question.

But, of course, questions can do much more than enquire: we can use them to spark an argument or to make ourselves look clever. Questions can be statements in disguise; we can use them to criticize, ridicule or even insult.

It is not always considered good form to ask questions. We may stop ourselves asking a question because we fear challenging authority, or looking stupid. In some organizations, asking questions is simply 'not done'. 'Questioning', said Samuel Johnson on one occasion, 'is not the mode of conversation among gentlemen.'

The best questions open up the speaker's thinking. A question that helps them to think further, develop an idea or clarify a thought, is a high-quality question. So use questions to:

- find out facts;
- check your understanding;
- help the other person to improve their understanding;
- invite the other person to examine your own thinking;
- request action.

A whole repertoire of questions is available to help you to enquire more fully. Specifically, we can use six types of questions:

- *Closed questions* can only be answered 'yes' or 'no'.
- *Leading questions* put the answer into the other person's mouth.
- *Controlling questions* help you to take the lead in the conversation.
- *Probing questions* build on an earlier question, or dig deeper.
- *Open questions* cannot be answered 'yes' or 'no'.

- *Reflecting questions* restate the last remark but with no new request.

Remember also the ladder of inference from Chapter 3. This powerful tool can provide all sorts of questions. You can also use it to invite the speaker to ask you questions.

One particular kind of question is especially powerful. It can liberate the speaker's thinking by removing the assumptions that limit it. This magic question starts with two words: 'What if'.

Guess an assumption that the speaker might be making and then ask either, 'What if this assumption weren't true?' or 'What if the opposite assumption were true?'

Examples of the first kind of question might include:

- *What if you became chief executive tomorrow?*
- *What if I weren't your manager?*
- *What if you weren't limited in your use of equipment?*

Examples of the second kind might include:

- *What if you weren't limited by a budget?*
- *What if customers were actually flocking to us?*
- *What if you knew that you were vital to the company's success?*

People are often inhibited from developing their thinking by two deep assumptions. One is that they are incapable of thinking well about something, or achieving something. The other is that they do not deserve to think well or achieve. Asking good questions can help you to encourage the other person to overcome these inhibitors and grow as a competent thinker.

EXERCISE

Next time you prepare for a fact-finding conversation – an appraisal interview, perhaps, or a project update – make a list of the questions you could ask. Try to include at least one of every type: closed, leading, controlling, probing, open, reflecting, 'what if'. Think about a possible order for these questions, and how some questions might be alternatives or potential questions, depending on the direction the conversation takes.

Rationing information

Information is power. Withholding information can be a power move, putting you at an advantage over the other person. But offering *too much* information can also interfere with enquiry: it can stop the other person thinking effectively. So it helps, in enquiry mode, to *ration* the information you give:

- *Don't interrupt.* Let the speaker finish before giving any new information. Don't force information into the middle of their sentence.

- *Time your intervention.* Ask yourself when the most appropriate time might be to offer the information.

- *Filter the information.* Only offer information that you think will improve the speaker's thinking. Resist the temptation to amplify some piece of information that is not central to the direction of their thinking.

- *Don't give information to show off.* You may be tempted to give information to demonstrate how expert or up to date you are. Resist that temptation.

You can also ration the amount of information you ask the speaker to give you. Ask for information at the right time and for the right reason; better to let the speaker work out their own ideas and then ask for a summary, than to keep interrupting them with questions.

Giving positive feedback

We use feedback to check that our enquiry has been successful. But feedback can do more: it can prepare us to switch the mode of conversation from enquiry to persuasion. It can also help us to end a conversation, summarizing your response to what the speaker has said and providing the foundations for a conversation for action.

Choose carefully when to give your feedback. If in doubt, ask whether it is appropriate to start your feedback or whether the speaker wants to continue. Ask:

- for permission to feed back;
- how the speaker sees the situation in summary;
- what the speaker sees as the key issue or problem.

Only then should you launch into your own feedback.

The best kind of feedback is *genuine*, *succinct* and *specific*. If you fake it, the other person will probably notice. If you go on too long, they will suspect your honesty. And if you are too general, they will find it hard to use the feedback.

Balancing appreciation and criticism

There are two kinds of feedback: positive and negative. The differences are obvious: positive feedback tells the other person what we like, and negative feedback tells them what we don't like.

Clearly the two kinds of feedback have different consequences. Positive feedback encourages the other person to go on thinking; negative feedback is likely to stop them thinking. But positive feedback also encourages the speaker to *value* their own thinking; negative feedback tells them that their thinking is worthless.

We often assume that negative feedback is more realistic than positive feedback. 'Get real', we might say to justify negative feedback. We might assume that positive feedback – saying what we like about an idea – is naive and simplistic. Years of training and experience in critical thinking may have taught you not to comment on what you approve or like.

Actually, of course, the positive aspects of reality can be just as realistic as the negative ones. Adding positive feedback to the negative does not distort our view of reality; it adds to it.

You can discover a source of positive feedback simply by asking yourself, 'What's good about this idea?' You could even ask the speaker the same question. The answer will nearly always reveal something that you had not noticed before. And that can form the basis for positive feedback.

Another way to transform negative into positive feedback is to use the phrase 'how to'. For example, if you want to say, 'We simply don't have the resources to do this', you could rephrase the remark by asking 'How could we do this with the limited resources we have?' If you want to say 'You haven't thought this through', you could ask 'How can we develop this idea more thoroughly?'

Those two simple words – 'how to' – can have a magical effect on the quality of your feedback.

EXERCISE

Spend one day noting down all your responses to ideas from other people. How many times were your comments negative – in other words, expressing what you didn't like about something or what you thought was wrong with the idea? How many comments were positive – expressing what you liked about the idea or what you thought was good about it? How could you transform the negative comments into positive ones? Could you, for example, turn a criticism into a 'how could we' question?

SUMMARY POINTS

- There are seven key skills of enquiry:
    - paying attention;
    - treating the speaker as an equal;
    - cultivating ease;
    - encouraging;
    - asking quality questions;
    - rationing information;
    - giving positive feedback.
- To pay attention:
    - listen;
    - don't interrupt;
    - allow quiet;
    - show that you are paying attention.
- To treat the speaker as an equal:
    - give equal turns to speak and listen;
    - don't tell them what to say;
    - don't assume that you know what they mean better than they do.
- To cultivate ease:
    - find time;
    - make space;
    - banish distractions.
- To encourage:
    - don't compete in the conversation;
    - explore differences of opinion;
    - use minimal encouragers.

- Ask quality questions to help you:
  - find out facts;
  - check your understanding;
  - help the other person to improve their understanding;
  - invite the other person to examine your own thinking;
  - request action.
- To ration information:
  - don't interrupt;
  - time your intervention;
  - filter the information;
  - don't give information to show off.
- To give positive feedback:
  - balance appreciation and criticism;
  - assume constructive intent;
  - feed back on specifics.

5 The skills of persuasion

The ability to persuade has never been in more demand. Anyone who can win hearts and minds will not be out of work for long. If communication begins with understanding, then it surely ends in persuasion.

This magical talent has been the subject of study for thousands of years. The classical Greeks called it *rhetoric*: the earliest manual that survives is by Aristotle. In the Middle Ages and the Renaissance, rhetoric was core curriculum in European schools and universities; Shakespeare's genius, for example, is underpinned by a solid rhetorical training.

These days, few of us study rhetoric; but the great tradition still has plenty to teach us about influencing and persuading. To return yet again to that first question – *What effect am I having?* – rhetoric teaches us how to employ a wide range of different effects.

In particular, rhetoric shows us that persuasion works both consciously and unconsciously. We might call the unconscious element 'influence'. (Vance Packard's famous 1957 book, *The Hidden Persuaders*, explored subliminal influence in advertising and the media.) The most successful persuasion will always include a great deal of influencing.

Character, logic and passion

Aristotle suggested that persuasion combined three skills. A speaker could appeal to his audience (in classical rhetoric, the speaker was almost always male) by establishing a good reputation with them, by using logic and by stirring their emotions. Aristotle famously named these three skills *ethos*, *logos* and *pathos*. He was writing about orators: politicians, lawyers and generals addressing huge crowds of Athenian citizens. But his model has just as much to teach a manager speaking at a meeting, or a call-centre team answering customer queries.

Character (ethos)

We tend to believe people we believe to be 'of good character' – people we trust or respect. *Ethos* is the skill of establishing that trust and fostering that respect. The key question in working on *ethos* is: why should your audience believe *you*?

Aristotle suggested that *ethos* itself comprises three skills:

- First, demonstrate that you share your audience's values. If you can show that your beliefs, priorities and attitudes align to those of your audience, they will feel that you're one of them.

- Second, display practical common sense. Indicate that you know something about how the real world operates, and that textbook solutions don't always work out in practice. Favour the middle way; reject extremes.

- And third, demonstrate that you have invested personally in the idea you're arguing for. What have you done to contribute to making this proposition successful? Better still, what have you sacrificed?

EXERCISE

The next time you're preparing to make a case to a manager or team, put the argument to one side briefly, and note down how you can increase your *ethos* with whoever you are seeking to persuade. How can you demonstrate that you share their values? How can you demonstrate practical good sense and moderation? How can you demonstrate a sense of personal commitment to your proposal?

Logic (logos)

Logic is apparently the work of rational thought, rather than unconscious influence. By using *logos*, we are appealing to our audience's ability to reason. We construct an argument by making a case, and creating reasons to support that case. Reasons are linked to the case by logic.

But logic is only *apparently* conscious and rational. Every argument is based on assumptions, and those assumptions – by definition – are unconscious. If your argument is based on assumptions that your audience doesn't share, then no amount of logical argumentation will succeed in persuading them. (More about logic later in this chapter.)

Passion (pathos)

Pathos persuades by appealing to the parts of our audience that rational argument cannot reach. The pathetic appeal is usually defined as an appeal to the emotions. Emotions provoke us to act without needing to think: that is why we say that we feel *moved* when in the grip of an emotion.

If we want to persuade, we *must* engage our audience's feelings. It may feel manipulative or dishonest, but ignoring the emotions is likely to seem cold and inhuman. (Mr Spock on *StarTrek* continually had this problem when trying to persuade his colleagues to act rationally.) Our rhetorical aim must be to stimulate the feeling appropriate to the action we want our audience to take.

Pathos, however, does more than arouse emotion. Anything that influences our audience unconsciously is part of the pathetic appeal. (There is more about the power of *pathos* later in this chapter, in the section on expressing your ideas.)

SIX PRINCIPLES OF INFLUENCE

Professor Robert Cialdini, in his bestseller *Influence: The science of persuasion*, identifies six patterns of influence, all of which operate unconsciously. Any one of them can enhance the pathetic appeal:

- *Reciprocity: the old give and take (and take)*
  We feel a strong urge to repay a favour. Offer your audience a gift – or a concession – and they may feel moved to do what you want.

- *Authority: directed deference*
  We are easily moved by people whose authority we recognize. (Here, *pathos* meets *ethos*.)

- *Scarcity: less is more*
  We are motivated to reach for something we think is in short supply. We are also motivated more by the prospect of losing something than gaining something. Point out what your audience might lose and you will strike an emotional chord.

- *Consistency: I am what I say*
  We want to be seen to be consistent with past behaviours. Show that what you want someone to do aligns with something they have done or said in the past.
- *Alignment: truths are us*
  We are strongly influenced to feel and do what we know people around us are feeling and doing. Persuading people as a group can often be more successful than seeking to persuade them individually.
- *Liking: I like you, you're like me*
  We would all prefer to say 'yes' to someone we know and like. Exploit your similarity to your audience: in your actions, in your words, even perhaps in the way you dress.

(Remember these six patterns with the mnemonic RASCAL.)

All three of these qualities – character, logic and passion – must be present if you want to persuade someone. The *process* of working out how to persuade them consists of five key elements:

- identifying the core idea;
- arranging your ideas logically;
- developing an appropriate style in the language you use;
- remembering your ideas;
- delivering your ideas with words, visual cues and non-verbal behaviour.

What's the Big Idea?

What do you want to say? A single idea is more likely to persuade your listener than a group of ideas, simply because one strong idea is easier to remember.

Take time to find that Big Idea. Conduct imaginary conversations in your head and note down the kind of things you might say. Now ask three questions:

- '*What is my objective?*' What do I want to achieve? What would I like to see happen?

- '*Who am I talking to?*' Why am I talking to this person about this objective? What do they already know? What more do they need to know? What do I want them to do? What ideas are likely to convince them?

- '*What is the most important thing I have to say to them?*' If I were only allowed a few minutes with them, what would I say? What if you had only a few *seconds* to get your Big Idea across? (Film executives call this 'the elevator pitch'. Imagine that you were in the lift with your listener for a few seconds between floors.)

Try to create a single sentence. You cannot express an idea without uttering a sentence. Does this sentence express what you want to say clearly and coherently?

Now test your Big Idea. If you were to speak this sentence to your listener, would they ask you a question? If you are arguing a point, you're looking for the question 'Why?'

You may need to prepare your listener for your Big Idea. To 'bring them around to your way of thinking', you may need to fill them in on some background, set the context or focus their attention. This means doing a bit of unconscious influencing: some *ethos*, perhaps, and a dash of *pathos*.

A neat way to pull all this together can be to tell a story. Biljana Scott, in a paper for the organization Diplo, puts it well:

> *The Greek concept of* pathos, *although defined as 'the appeal to emotion for rhetorical effect', tends to include within its remit imagination, identification and a sense of fellow suffering*

(pathos means both 'suffering' and 'experience'); all defining components of a gripping story.

Here is a simple four-point structure that you can use to construct that story. I remember it by using the letters SPQR (which is the motto of the Roman Empire).

Situation

Briefly tell the listener something they already know. You are showing that you understand their situation and can appreciate their point of view. (That's *ethos* at work.) You are also showing that you identify with them. (There's the touch of *pathos*.) Think of the Situation statement as a kind of 'Once upon a time...'. It sets the scene for the rest of the story.

Problem

Now identify a Problem that has arisen within the Situation. The Problem complicates the Situation in some way: it sets up the tension without which you wouldn't have a story.

Unlike the Situation, the Problem will probably be new information for your listener. And it should make them pay attention. This is something they need to know about. It really should be *their* problem.

Problems come in all shapes and sizes. Something may have gone wrong, or be threatening to go wrong. Something may have changed (or not changed). We may not know what to do; we may be facing a range of options from which we must choose.

Don't forget the *pathos* at this point. Negative problems might arouse fear or concern; opportunities should arouse a sense of excitement.

Question

The Problem should prompt your listener to ask a Question. What question would you like them to ask? Presumably, the Question that allows you to deliver your Big Idea. Tell the story to maximize your chances that your listener asks that very Question.

What's the Question?

SITUATION	PROBLEM	QUESTION
Stable, agreed status quo	Something has gone wrong	What do we do?
	Something could go wrong	How do we stop it?
	Something has changed	How do we adjust to it?
	Something could change	How do we prepare for it?
	Something new has arisen	What can we do?
	Someone has a different point of view	Who is right?
	We don't know what to do	What do we do? (or) How do we choose?
	There are a number of things we could do	Which course do we take?

Response

Your Response to the Question should be your Big Idea. Your listener should now be ready to consider that idea because it answers a question that *they* have asked.

SPQR is a classic storytelling framework. It is also well known as a method that management consultants use in the introductions to their proposals. The trick is to tell the story *quickly*. Don't be tempted to fill out the story with lots of detail. Focus on what interests the listener. You're influencing them, not yet persuading them. Keep your listener's attention by reflecting what they know, as well as their values, priorities and concerns.

Arranging your ideas logically

Logic is the glue that binds ideas into arguments. In its most basic form, an argument consists of three elements:

- a *claim* (the point you are arguing for);
- a *reason* (a statement that supports the claim);
- and the word '*because*'.

All the logic in your argument is tied up in that simple word: *because*. And even the logic of your argument has an unconscious element.

Finding the warrant

Every argument is based on assumptions. Surfacing and testing those assumptions is a critical step in constructing a persuasive argument.

Let's take a very simple argument and analyse it. If you say 'Eat more vegetables because they're good for you', the statement before '*because*' is your claim, and the statement after it is your reason.

How persuasive is this argument? It depends who you are trying to persuade.

In any argument, the connection between claim and reason is based on an assumption. If we agree with the assumption that we should always do what is good for our health, then we are likely to accept the argument that we should eat more vegetables. A medical student, for example, might accept the assumption but then demand evidence that vegetables are indeed good for us. A child, in contrast, is unlikely to share the assumption that we should always do what is good for us – and with them, the argument is likely to fail.

This underlying assumption, connecting the reason to the claim, is sometimes called a *warrant*. If your listener shares the warrant underlying your argument, you have a good chance of persuading them. But if they don't share that assumption, the argument could fail. Many logical arguments fail – in the home, in the media and in the workplace – because the audience doesn't share the warrant that underlies them. We see this mismatch most vividly in political or religious arguments, but you will spot it also in business meetings, interviews and sales conversations. If you are arguing a case, pay close attention to the assumptions that underlie it. Does your audience share those assumptions?

Expressing your ideas

When we express our ideas, we need to combine the rational *logos* of our argument with the emotional and imaginative appeal of *pathos*. Pictures may work better than words: if you want your audience to donate to an animal charity, show them a picture of an animal in distress (better still, bring an animal on stage with you). The appeal to the senses is not restricted to visual images, of course; think about how any of the five senses might respond to your Big Idea.

Examples

Perhaps the simplest way to bring an idea alive is to offer a concrete example. Audiences are more likely to be persuaded by a single example than a raft of statistics. A good example will also show that you know your stuff, and that you can apply it to real life (a key element of *ethos*.) Find an instance where the idea has been put into practice, or where it has created real results – either useful or disastrous.

Convincing examples have three key characteristics:

- First, they usually include real people doing real things. Can you give an example of someone doing something that illustrates your Big Idea?

- Second, they include vivid description, which stimulates one or more of the five senses. What does this example sound like, look like, feel, smell or taste like?

- And third, convincing examples involve feeling or emotion. Talk about how pleased the client was, how relieved you were, how excited you are by this idea.

Using metaphors

Metaphors can be powerful persuaders. As we saw towards the end of Chapter 3, metaphors express one thing in terms of another; by linking a topic to something the listener already knows about, you create a bridge that allows them to cross over into your thinking.

You could use a single metaphor to capture your listener's imagination or stimulate their feelings. You can also use them in a more extended way, to explain a complicated or unusual topic. But if you do intend to use a metaphor in this extended way, you need to think carefully about the metaphor you choose.

The best metaphors clarify complex topics, rather than confusing the listener. They allow the listener to think more deeply or widely about the topic. For example, Dana Meadows, one of the gurus of systems theory, explains feedback loops using the metaphor of filling a glass with water. You turn on the tap, you watch the water level rise, and as it nears the top of the glass you regulate the flow of water. When the glass is full, you turn off the tap. This metaphor allows us to think more widely about feedback loops. For example, if you cannot see the glass, or if the flow of water is too fast, you will find operating the feedback loop more tricky.

To find the right metaphor, start with your audience:

- What do you know about what they know?

- What do you want them to be able to do as a result of understanding the topic?

- What aspects of your topic do you want to explain?
- What else in the world shares the qualities you are trying to explain?
- Experiment with the metaphor and see how far you can extend it.
- Review your choice. Are you making the topic easier to understand?

Remembering your ideas

Memory played a vital role in the art of rhetoric in the days before printing. With no ready means of making notes and no easy access to books, orators had to remember what to say, and in what order. Whole systems of memory were invented to help them.

These days, the art of memory has been replaced by technology – except, perhaps, for passing examinations. We have no *need* to remember; merely to read and store e-mails, pick up messages on the mobile, plug in, surf and download.

But memory still plays an important part in persuading others. No one was ever persuaded by watching someone recite from a sheaf of notes.

Find a way to bring the ideas off paper and into your head. Give yourself some clear mental signposts so that you can find your way from one idea to the next. Have a way of *showing* your thoughts as you explain them: a notepad, a flipchart, a whiteboard. Invite the other person to join in: encourage them to think of this as the shape of *their* thinking.

EXERCISE

The next time you're preparing a presentation, find time to draw a picture of it. Put all your notes away; you are working from memory here. Find as large a piece of paper as possible, and pens or pencils of different colours, and draw the presentation as a journey, or perhaps a storyboard (like a strip cartoon, the kind of drawings that film-makers use to map out a sequence of shots). You are aiming for a single route through the material. Put memorable stopping places along the way: signposts, buildings, statues, posters, etc. Now use your drawing to help you rehearse.

Delivering effectively

You are as much a part of the persuasive process as your argument, your examples and your stories. If you're saying one thing but your body is saying another, no one will believe your words.

Start, as ever, with the person you are trying to persuade. Do they favour a relaxed, informal conversational style, or a more formal, presentational delivery? Are they interested in the broad picture or lots of supporting detail? Will they want to ask questions?

Delivery is broadly about three kinds of activity. Think about the way you use your: eyes, voice and body.

Effective eye contact

We speak more with our eyes than with our voices. Maintain eye contact with your listener. If you are talking to more than one person, include everyone with your eyes. Focus on their eyes; don't look through them.

Using your voice

Your voice will sound more persuasive if it is not too high, too fast or too thin. Regulate and strengthen your breathing while you speak. Breathe deep and slow. Let your voice emerge more from your body than from your throat. The more body that your voice has, and the more measured your vocal delivery, the more convincing you will sound.

You will find more tips on breathing in Chapter 7. Meanwhile, try this exercise.

EXERCISE

Here's how to find the best version of your voice. (Thanks to Caroline Goyder for this exercise.) Put your thumb just below where your ribs separate (just below where the front of a bra strap goes – if you wear one). You are feeling for a layer of muscle: massage it gently and feel it soften. Now gently tap that point and let out a big belly laugh. Or yawn loudly. Feel how the sound of your voice drops down and becomes more relaxed. Jump up and down and speak. Become aware of how your voice is coming from your centre – almost up from your lower spine. *That's* the voice you're looking for. Everyone has it; we just need to find it. Once you have done this exercise, try singing what you want to say. Listen to how your voice shifts between speaking and singing. You are aiming to locate the source of your voice between your chest and your stomach – not your throat.

Persuasive body language

Your face, your limbs and your body posture will all contribute to the total persuasive effect. Keep your facial muscles moving and your neck muscles relaxed. Use your hands to paint pictures, to help you find the right words and express yourself fully.

Professional persuaders observe their listeners' behaviour and quietly mirror it. If you are relaxed with the other person, that mirroring will tend to happen naturally: you may find you are crossing your legs in similar ways or moving your arms in roughly the same way. Try consciously to adapt your own posture and movement to that of your listener. Do more: take the lead. Don't sit back or close your body off when you are seeking to persuade; bring yourself forward, open yourself up and present yourself, along with your ideas.

SUMMARY POINTS

- We can persuade by using:
  - *ethos*: appealing to our audience's sense of our character or reputation;
  - *logos*: appealing to their reason;
  - *pathos*: appealing to their emotions.
- *Ethos* is the appeal to our audience through:
  - personality;
  - reputation;
  - personal credibility.
- *Logos* uses two forms of logic:
  - deductive;
  - inductive.

▶

- *Pathos* is the appeal to emotions or feelings:
  - The pathetic appeal must always be indirect.
  - Pathos should never be dishonest.
  - Provoke the feeling that is appropriate to the action you want the audience to take.
- The *process* of working out how to persuade them consists of five key elements:
  - Identifying the core idea.
  - Arranging your ideas logically.
  - Developing an appropriate style in the language you use.
  - Remembering your ideas.
  - Delivering your ideas with words, visual cues and non-verbal behaviour.
- To identify the core idea, ask:
  - 'What is my objective?'
  - 'Who am I talking to?'
  - 'What is the most important thing I have to say to them?'
- The message sentence should be:
  - a single idea;
  - no longer than about 15 words long;
  - action-centred;
  - self-contained;
  - attention-grabbing.
- To arrange your ideas logically:
  - Ask what question your message provokes: 'Why?' 'How?' 'Which ones?'
  - Use SPQR to introduce your message and fill in the background.
  - Use deductive or inductive logic to arrange your supporting ideas.

- To express your ideas more vividly, use:
  - images;
  - examples;
  - metaphors.
- To remember your material, use visual aids such as:
  - mind maps;
  - flipcharts;
  - whiteboards.
- And to deliver your ideas well:
  - maintain effective eye contact;
  - use your voice well;
  - make your body language persuasive.

6 Tough conversations

At some point at work, you will have to hold a tough conversation. It goes, as they say, with the territory. Any book about improving your communication skills should help you with the conversations you struggle with. (Of course, we also have to hold tough conversations outside work. This book focuses on communication in the workplace, but the skills we discuss are applicable in personal conversations too.)

To misquote Tolstoy: all happy conversations are alike; all tough conversations are tough in their own way. When conversations go well, it is usually for similar reasons: rapport is high, we are talking the same language, and the conversation's objective is clear. In contrast, conversations can become tough for different reasons. Some are predictable; many take us completely by surprise.

Six tough conversations

Holly Weeks, adjunct lecturer in public policy at Harvard Kennedy School, sets out six broad types of tough conversation in her book, *Failure to Communicate*. You will probably recognize all six:

- *I've got bad news.* Every manager, at some point, will need to tell someone something they don't want to hear.

- *You're challenging my power.* The opposite, in some ways, of the previous conversation: you need to raise a problem with your manager, and you are worried that they may feel threatened.
- *I can't go there.* If you are conflict-averse, you may try to avoid the tough conversation – and make it tougher.
- *You win/I lose.* You are trying to be cooperative and the other person insists on making it competitive – and trying to win.
- *What's going on here?* A calm conversation suddenly becomes charged with negative emotion. Perhaps an innocent remark has been taken entirely the wrong way, with catastrophic consequences.
- *I'm being attacked.* The other person in the conversation suddenly starts accusing, shouting, threatening or being abusive.

What makes conversations tough?

Difficult conversations become tough when they develop three features. First, we sense – sometimes suddenly, shockingly – that we don't understand what is going on. In particular, we have no idea why our counterpart in the conversation is behaving as they are. Second, emotion rears its head, clouding our judgement and dictating all sorts of unhelpful tactics. Among those tactics is the third key feature of a tough conversation: conflict.

Each of these three elements can cause us to choose tactics that can make the conversation tougher.

The fog of uncertainty

A conversation becomes tough when we cannot see what is happening. In particular, we find it impossible to read our counterpart's intentions. As a result, we make assumptions about those intentions – and those assumptions tend to take a predictable form. All too often, we allocate blame.

Blame is, in fact, a completely natural and understandable reaction to uncertainty. Faced with a situation that we don't understand, we will tend to assume that it has been created by someone – or something – *deliberately*. We might blame the gods for natural catastrophes; we construct conspiracy theories to explain extraordinary tragedies. We blame, even when there is no one obvious to blame: we shout at the computer when it crashes, we kick a burst tyre. In a conversation, blame is a natural response to behaviour we cannot read clearly.

As well as finding it impossible to read the other person's intentions, we find it hard to read their reactions to what we are saying. Mostly, we can exercise what psychologists call a theory of mind: we can infer the thoughts and feelings of the other person by reading their behaviour. In a tough conversation, the readings we pick up from the other person's gestures, facial expressions and verbal responses fail to add up: they are confusing or contradictory. Something is not quite right, but we cannot work out what it is.

Emotional arousal

Faced with these uncertainties, our minds tend to respond emotionally.

Think of your brain as being like an office building with three floors. (This explanation of brain function – it is called the *triune brain* – is grossly simplified but nonetheless helpful.) In the basement (usually called the brain stem) are the control systems for the body's vital functions: heart rate, breathing, body temperature, balance and so on. On the ground floor – it is actually in the centre of the brain – is the limbic system, which acts as a kind of reception area for all the information that enters the brain. Sitting at the front desk in the limbic system is the amygdala, which we can think of as a kind of security officer. The amygdala has a very simple job: it gives incoming information a visitor's badge, in the form of an emotional tag. If the visitor is welcome, the amygdala sends it up to the top floor of the brain, the neocortex, which can think more subtly and intelligently about the information.

But if the amygdala decides that the information is unwelcome, it will tag it as dangerous. It's like a security alert. And the first thing that happens in a security alert, of course, is that the lifts are closed down. No more shuttling between floors; no more subtle, intelligent thinking. The limbic system cuts off all neural connections to the neocortex and calls in the emotions to deal with the threat. We call this *emotional arousal*: in the words of Daniel Goleman, author of *Emotional Intelligence*, the limbic system hijacks the neocortex. It is a survival mechanism, helping us to deal with a situation *without thinking about it*.

The problem, of course, is that this emotional arousal only serves to make a tough conversation tougher. The emotions – the fear, anger or embarrassment – are telling us to act: to do something *now*, without stopping to think. The limbic system has reduced our options to just two: run away, or fight it out. Hence the name: the *fight-or-flight response*.

The combat mentality

If one person in a conversation is experiencing the fight-or-flight response, the conversation is likely to become difficult. The other person may have to use all their skill to reduce their emotional arousal and cancel the security alert in their brain. But all too often, faced with aggressive behaviour, our own limbic systems respond to the threat – and what Holly Weeks calls the combat mentality is established. A difficult conversation has become tough.

The combat mentality treats the conversation as a battle. Every move is seen as an unprovoked attack, and the only strategy available to our brains – locked down in that limbic security alert – is to defend or attack. The combat mentality can cause real damage: bruising emotional wounds that can leave permanent scars on a working relationship.

How we make tough conversations tougher

These three elements – uncertainty, emotional arousal, the combat mentality – act together. Between them, they create a self-reinforcing, vicious cycle. As it spirals out of control, we feel increasingly powerless to intervene. We may want to save the conversation; we may even be able to see what is going wrong. But we cannot think about what to do. Instead, the cycle dictates our behaviour.

First, as we have seen, we blame the other person for the problem. And in blaming them, we assume ourselves to be innocent. That assumption of innocence can become what Holly Weeks calls 'the delusion of good intentions': the idea that tough conversations shouldn't happen to us, because we mean well and we always try to do our best. It's a delusion because it does not take account of how we might be contributing to our counterpart's behaviour.

Our resulting strategy is that we evade responsibility for the conversation. We justify what we do as the inevitable result of what *they* are doing, and *only* what they are doing. Second, emotional arousal leads us to oversimplify the problem. Simplifying our thinking is one of the prime functions of emotions: they make it easier for us to choose what to do. In fact, we *don't* choose what to do; the emotion chooses for us.

Our resulting strategies respond to the oversimplified problem by forcing an oversimplified solution. The emotions force us into black-and-white thinking: this or that, good or bad. We might try to force through an either/or decision: yes or no, your way or my way, take it or leave it. Or we might go for the generalizing strategy: this is always what happens when we discuss this issue, it is always bad, and this is what we always do to deal with it.

And third, the combat mentality dictates a whole host of strategies. Battles have only two outcomes: win or lose. Once we have taken on the combat mentality, every move must aim to win. We might seek to dictate terms, or engage in confrontational argument.

And we might engage in what Holly Weeks calls 'thwarting ploys'. The aim of these ploys, she writes, 'is to get us to back off, to make our counterparts themselves come out on top, or to get out of the conversation altogether'.

Thwarting ploys come in all shapes and sizes. Some are defensive, some offensive; some manage to be both. They might include:

- bursting into tears;
- laughing off a derogatory remark as a joke;
- pleading external duties that make it impossible to stop and talk;
- switching the topic of conversation unexpectedly.

The most successful thwarting ploys have one feature in common: they are hard to read. We have come full circle, back to that first key feature of tough conversations: the fog of uncertainty. Thwarting ploys add to the uncertainty; that's why we use them. What's worse, when we spot a thwarting ploy, we often assume that we know why the other person is using it. But of course, we might be wrong. Is the other person wilfully, or genuinely, misunderstanding what we say? Are they evading the issue or simply changing the subject? Are they upset or putting it on?

Three steps towards better tough conversations

How can we break this cycle? Given the complexity of tough conversations – the fog of uncertainty, the swirl of emotion, the smoke of combat – can we find tactics that are simple enough to remember and practise?

Holly Weeks suggests that our strategy should begin with three-way respect. We should respect ourselves, the other person and the conversation itself.

Self-respect, to begin with, means paying attention to our own needs.

WHAT HUMANS NEED

We all have needs that we must meet in order to function as effective human beings. Some needs are physical; others are psychological.

PHYSICAL NEEDS	PSYCHOLOGICAL NEEDS
Air	Security
Water	Attention
Nutritious food	A sense of autonomy and control
Sleep	Emotional connections to others
Sensory stimulation	Membership of a community
Physical exercise	Friendship, fun, love, intimacy
Shelter	Sense of status in social situations
Safety	Sense of competence and achievement
	Meaning and purpose:
	– people who need us
	– activities that stretch us (flow; peak experiences that focus our attention; being 'in the zone')
	– connection to a bigger picture

A conversation can become tough if one of us feels that something in the conversation threatens a need. If you sense resistance – either in yourself or in the other person – ask yourself, 'What need is being threatened here?'

This model of human needs is based on the Human Givens approach, pioneered by Joe Griffin and Ivan Tyrrell.

Self-respect means meeting our needs. Among the most important of those needs are:

- Competence: the sense that we are good at what we do.
- Autonomy: the sense that we are in control of our lives.
- Relatedness: the sense that we are connected to others.

(The mnemonic 'CAR' will help you to remember these three core needs.) Meeting our needs does not mean ignoring the needs of others. Neither does it mean using thwarting ploys to protect our need. A ploy is likely to protect us only in the short term; self-respect means knowing that we need to meet our needs more fully and deeply.

Respect for the other person means acknowledging that they, too, have the same needs that we have. Respecting our counterpart does not mean that we must agree with them or give way to them. Neither does it mean that we should like them. It means simply that we should recognize that they have needs and interests of their own.

Of course, part of what they are doing is responding to what *we* are saying and doing. It may be extremely important to them, for example, not to lose face: not to be embarrassed or humiliated publicly. So respecting the other person also means seeking to understand how our behaviour might be affecting their self-esteem. (*What effect am I having?*) This means understanding our own behaviour more deeply. Thus, respect for ourselves and for the other person reinforce each other.

Finally, respecting the conversation means recognizing it for what it is: tough. Holly Weeks suggests that we view a tough conversation as a landscape, to be navigated. 'Rather than put our heads down and start to plough through', she writes, 'we will do better to step back, take a satellite view and think about the lay of the land.' We are looking for an effective route through the obstacles that this conversation is likely to throw up.

How does this three-way respect play out in practice? What can we *do*?

We could start by considering the context of the conversation. Do you need to act on either of these questions?

- *Time.* Is this the right time? What is the history behind the conversation?
- *Place.* Are you somewhere comfortable, quiet, and – perhaps above all – private?

If you pick the right time and the right place, the conversation has a better chance of turning out better. And there are other tactics we could choose to try.

But we do need to *choose* what to do. A tough conversation is unlikely to improve by chance. The three elements – the fog of uncertainty, emotional arousal and the combat mentality – act as a mutually reinforcing cycle. We can start anywhere in the cycle. But we need to start somewhere. And only *we* can choose to act. We cannot predict what the other person does, and we may not be able to control their behaviour directly. But we can influence their behaviour by what we do. It's up to us.

Clearing the fog of uncertainty

If we want to reduce uncertainty in a tough conversation, we need more information. We need to use all the skills of enquiry that we can muster.

A good first step is to banish blame. As we have seen, blame encourages us to believe that the other person's intentions are hostile towards us. If we simply reverse this assumption, we open up new possibilities for gaining information.

The principle is: *assume constructive intent.* (We have mentioned this tactic before, at the end of Chapter 4.) Assume that the other person is doing what they are doing, and saying what they are saying, for good reasons: reasons that make sense to them. They are trying to meet their needs for competence, autonomy or relatedness, in some way. Assume, also, that they may not *know* precisely why they are doing what they're doing.

It is possible, even in the threatening confusion of a tough conversation, to make this very simple move. But assuming constructive intent will be easier if you have practised the skill beforehand.

EXERCISE

Assuming constructive intent

Try this whenever you are relaxed and able to observe someone's behaviour without feeling threatened by it. (Meetings are good opportunities to do this exercise. You might be observing two people discussing an issue, without participating directly yourself.) The moment to watch for is when someone disagrees with a remark or seems to show resistance. Ask yourself the question: 'What good reason might they have for resisting or disagreeing?' Test your thinking using the three needs we have mentioned: competence, autonomy, relatedness. Is it possible that one of these needs is being threatened? How could you find out, if you were taking part in this conversation?

The next move is to ask questions. A really powerful information-gathering tool is the ladder of inference. Look back at Chapter 3: you will find plenty of questions there that will help you to climb down the ladder of inference and explore the beliefs and facts underlying what your counterpart is saying.

We often go into conversations knowing that they will be difficult. In those cases, we can plan the questioning strategy to help us clear the fog of uncertainty. The trick is to have lots of questions ready, and be ready to change direction at any point. Plan, but don't script.

Reducing emotional arousal

That tangled thicket of emotions is probably the greatest obstacle in your path through a tough conversation. Although we are looking at emotions as the second element of tough conversations, you may need to tackle emotional arousal first, before you can make any more progress.

Why can emotions be so disabling? Because they stop us thinking clearly. That is their natural function (and this bears repeating): emotions tell us how to act *without thinking*. (Look back at the notes on *pathos* in Chapter 5. E-*motions* provoke *motion*.) Tough conversations, more than any others, need us to think clearly. Extreme, negative emotions get in the way of clear thinking.

How can we reduce emotional arousal? You will have to work on yourself before trying to influence the other person. The first step is to focus on your breathing. Take a couple of deep breaths and try to breathe *out* for longer than you breathe *in*. (This technique is called *7/11 breathing*. You will find an exercise in Chapter 7 that explains it in more detail.) You should have plenty of time to work on your breathing while listening to the other person answering your questions; if you cannot seem to find the space to breathe for a moment, you may be talking too much!

Now slow the conversation down. Review the material in Chapter 3 on managing time. A very effective way to slow the pace of the conversation is to work on your voice: lower the volume, lower the pitch and lower the pace. The effect on the other person can be magical: it is very hard to counter the effect of a soothing voice. But you will have to practise the technique so that you can engage it when you need to; the emotion of a tough conversation will be working hard against you.

You can alter your breathing and your voice in a matter of seconds. Now focus on the words of the conversation. If you repeat and paraphrase what your counterpart has been saying, you will discharge some of the emotion.

For example, if your counterpart says 'The sales targets are just too high', you could paraphrase by saying: 'So let me get this right. Are you saying that the sales targets have been set too high?' The paraphrase – especially if posed as a question – gives your counterpart the opportunity to reflect on their thinking, develop it or examine it. Paraphrasing can help both of you to think more objectively about the problem.

Paraphrasing can also slow down a conversation and instil a little calm – a tough conversation is unlikely to become relaxed, but at least you will now have the chance to navigate it more successfully.

From conflict to collaboration

Collaboration means working together to navigate the landscape of the conversation. One way to do that is to take a 'satellite view' of the conversation's subject.

Try running a 'how to' exercise. The technique is almost ridiculously simple: we define the problem as a phrase beginning with the words 'how to'. Invite the other person to join you in creating a 'how to' statement that defines the problem you are discussing. Offer your own 'how to' if you wish, and spend some time generating new, alternative 'how to' statements: different ways of defining the problem, different views of the problem, parts of the problem. Questions that will help you to generate more 'how to' statements include:

- What are we trying to achieve here?
- What do you want to do?
- If we could do this, what other problem would that solve?
- What do we need to do in order to do this?

Writing down the 'how to' statements will help you to objectify the problem still further. Sticky notes are useful: write each 'how to' on a separate note and start clustering them. By visualizing the problem in this way, you give yourself a greater opportunity to collaborate on solving it.

'How to' is a powerful first-stage thinking technique. (Look back at the section on structuring your thinking in Chapter 3.) It works particularly well as part of the second conversation in the sequence of four that we explored in Chapter 3: the conversation for possibility.

Edward de Bono, as we have seen in Chapter 3, calls conflict 'adversarial thinking'. According to de Bono, there are four main types of adversarial thinking:

- Critical thinking: looking for what is wrong with an idea.
- Ego thinking: identifying ourselves with our idea, so that attacking the idea becomes a personal attack.
- Political thinking: using ideas to create allies or destroy alliances.
- Rigid thinking: simplifying and reducing complexity so that ideas become impossible to develop or change.

You may be able to detect one or more of these types of thinking in the tough conversation you're holding. If so, these questions may help to defuse conflict and increase the chances of collaboration:

- To counter critical thinking, ask: 'What is good about this idea?'
- To counter ego thinking, ask: 'When does this happen? In what circumstances does this idea *not* apply?'
- To counter political thinking, ask: 'What are the strengths and weaknesses of this idea?'
- To counter rigid thinking, ask: 'What if...? What if... happened? What if... were not happening? What if... you could solve this problem?'

Tough conversations demand more than good intentions. They demand clear thinking, a clear strategy and clear tactics. Navigating a tough conversation does not mean ignoring the needs of the other person, but neither does it mean giving way or running away. We may not be able to understand or influence the other person's behaviour in a tough conversation – that is part of what makes it tough – but we can alter our own behaviour. The techniques we have explored in this chapter help us to improve the prospects for a tough conversation by acting on our side.

These techniques have one thing in common. We need to practise them before we need to use them. We can try out most of them in conversations that are not tough. Once we understand how they can help us, we will be ready whenever a conversation becomes tough.

SUMMARY POINTS

- Tough conversations have three key features:
  - the fog of uncertainty, particularly in reading our counterpart's intentions;
  - emotional arousal;
  - a combat mentality.
- We can make tough conversations tougher by making poor tactical choices:
  - The fog of uncertainty encourages us to blame the counterparty for the problem, and creates a delusion of good intentions.
  - Emotional arousal causes us to oversimplify the problem and seek oversimplified solutions: forced either/or decisions, or generalized judgements.

- The combat mentality provokes many strategies, including thwarting ploys.
- We can only manage tough conversations better if we respect ourselves, the other person and the conversation itself:
  - Self-respect means understanding our own needs and working to meet them.
  - Respecting the other person means remembering their needs and that they are trying to meet them.
  - Respecting the conversation means thinking about it as a landscape to be navigated together.
- We can adopt a number of techniques to break the cycle of a tough conversation:
  - We can clear the fog of uncertainty by assuming constructing intent, asking questions and using the ladder of inference.
  - We can reduce emotional arousal by working on our breathing and our voice, and by paraphrasing our counterpart's remarks before responding to them.
  - We can transform combat into collaboration by using the 'how to' technique, and by responding carefully to the four forms of adversarial thinking: critical thinking, ego thinking, political thinking and rigid thinking.
- Tough conversations demand more than good intentions. They demand clear thinking, a clear strategy and clear tactics. We need to practise these techniques before finding ourselves in a tough conversation.

7 Making a presentation

Think of a presentation as a formal conversation. It is a largely one-way conversation with a few specific rules: you are speaking, and the audience is supposed to be listening. You're leading; they are following. It's not the most natural of conversations. And that is where the challenges begin.

A recent study in the United States asked people about their deepest fears. Intriguingly, death came in at number seven. At the top of the list – above deep water, financial problems, insects and heights – was speaking to groups.

Why the anxiety? I think it is because, when we present, we put ourselves on show. The audience will be judging not just our ideas, but *us*. People may not easily remember reports or spreadsheets; but they will certainly remember a presenter who looks nervous or incompetent.

That nervous, jittery feeling is caused by adrenalin, a hormone secreted by your adrenal glands (near your kidneys). Adrenalin constricts your arteries, increasing your blood pressure and stimulating the heart. Why stimulate the heart? To give you extra energy. And when do you need extra energy? When you are in danger.

Adrenalin release is an evolved response to threat. It is all part of the fight-or-flight response, which helps us to confront or run away from life-threatening situations. Symptoms include a rapid pulse (to keep the blood well oxygenated), dilated pupils (so that we can see better) and sweaty palms (to help us grip a weapon).

That adrenalin rush has two other effects. It increases your concentration – particularly useful when making a presentation. Less usefully, adrenalin also stimulates excretion of body waste. This decreases your body weight, helping you to run faster. And *that* is why you want to visit the toilet immediately before presenting.

But the worst of it is that the audience will forget virtually everything you say.

That's the bad news.

The good news is that nervousness can help you to present more effectively. It is telling you that this presentation matters – and that *you* matter. An effective presenter puts themselves centre-stage; so you have every right to feel nervous. In fact, you *should* feel nervous. Your task is to *manage* those nerves.

EXERCISE

The best way to deal with nerves is to work on your breathing. Find somewhere comfortable to sit and relax. Relax your shoulders and put your hands on your stomach. Breathe in and out, if you can, through your nose: breathe in for a count of seven and out for a count of eleven. If these counts are too high, start with lower numbers – 3/6 perhaps – and work up towards 7/11. The important thing is to breathe *out* for longer than you breathe *in*. Check your shoulders: they should be remaining still. Check your hands: they should be gently pushing your stomach *out* as you breathe in, and falling back into your stomach as you breathe out. It may help to close your eyes and concentrate on counting as you do this exercise. (Combine this with the exercise on using your voice in Chapter 5.)

Breathing in and out at a count of 7/11 is brilliant for calming nerves and reducing anxiety. Breathing in quickens the heartbeat and stimulates adrenalin production; breathing out does the opposite, slowing the heart and the production of adrenalin. We tend to breathe in too much when we are anxious; 7/11 breathing simply reverses the connection, so that our breathing makes us less anxious. Practising 7/11 breathing also helps us to worry less, by forcing us to concentrate simply on our breathing.

Preparing for the presentation

Those nerves also reflect the uncertainty of a live presentation. The Greeks called this element *kairos*, a word that translates roughly as 'the opportune moment'.

The effective presenter understands that their presentation will be affected by a host of uncontrollable factors. You can't plan for the audience's mood. You may not even be able to foresee who will be there. You can't plan for any sudden external development that might affect your topic. You can't plan for every question that you might be asked.

But that, of course, is also the greatest strength of a presentation. You and the audience are together, in the same place, at the same time. This is a unique moment. You can respond to the *kairos*, if, as the Greeks did, you see it as an opportunity.

EXERCISE

What will affect the *kairos* the next time you make a presentation? Spend a little time thinking about the specific circumstances you will be working with: the audience's mood, what has been happening to them recently, events in the outside world that will be on their minds. How can you adapt your presentation to acknowledge or address those factors?

If you can support your nerves with solid preparation, you can channel your nervous energy into the performance itself. Prepare in three areas:

- the material;
- the audience;
- yourself.

Managing the material

Your most important task is to hold the audience's attention.

Presentations fail for many reasons. Perhaps the most common problem is that the presenter talks *about* something, rather than talking *to the audience*.

Other presentations fail because the presenter organizes the material as if it is a document. A presentation is not a report – or a set of slides. It needs to be structured like a performance: a story, a comedy routine, a piece of music. That performing structure must take the audience on a journey, with lots of interesting twists and turns along the way to hold their attention.

Defining your objective

Why are you presenting? What do you want your audience to *do* at the end? Your objective must be to say whatever is necessary to persuade them to take that action.

In other words, presentations are ideal for *influencing* and *persuading* an audience. On the whole, a presentation is not a good medium for *explaining* something. It is worth repeating this point: your audience is probably going to forget almost everything you say. So packing your presentation full of information – on slides, or anywhere else – is almost certainly counterproductive. If your brief is to explain something, try to find some persuasive element that will inject passion and purpose into the presentation. And if you *must* offer your audience detailed information, put it in supporting notes.

I believe that there is only one reason why you should be making a presentation. It may sound rather grand, but a presentation should *inspire* your audience. They want to be moved, involved, intrigued. Above all, they want to feel that they can *identify* with you and your ideas. They also want to identify with each other: that they are, for the brief time that this presentation lasts, a single community. Your task is to create in your audience that multiple sense of identification – with you, with your ideas and with themselves – so that they will be inspired to act.

Write down your objective in one sentence. This helps you to:

- clear your mind;
- select material to fit;
- check at the end of planning that you are still addressing a single clear issue.

Write a simple sentence beginning:

'The aim of this presentation is to...'

Make sure the verb following that word 'to' is suitably inspirational!

Analysing your audience

Your presentation will be successful if the audience feels that you have spoken directly to them. If your ideas directly address their needs, they will pay much more attention to them. Remember the skills of *ethos*, which we explored in Chapter 5? If you can show that you share the audience's values, that you value practical common sense and the middle way, and that you have made a personal investment in your ideas, your audience will respect you. And if they respect you, they will be more inclined to believe you.

So think about your audience carefully:

- How many will there be?
- What is their status range?
- Will they want to be there?
- How much do they already know about the matter? How much more do they need to know?
- How does your message and your material relate to the audience? Is the audience young or old? Are they predominantly one gender or mixed?
- Is the audience young or old? Are they predominantly one gender or mixed?

Your audience has certain expectations – of you and of itself. They will expect you to be competent, to set the pace and direction of the presentation, and to stay in control. They will expect themselves to be led, to be told what to think and feel, and to respond as a single group. Audiences can respond actively in presentations in only a few ways. They can interrupt you – to ask a question, to contradict you or to heckle you; they can laugh; and they can applaud. Your audience will expect you to manage these responses.

Constructing a message

Once you have your objective, and some sense of who your audience is, you can plan your material.

Work out your message. Look back at our notes on messages in Chapter 5. Your presentation's message must:

- be a sentence;
- express your objective;
- contain a single idea;
- have no more than 15 words;
- grab your audience's attention.

Make your message as vivid as you can. An effective message – in a presentation, we can call it the 'take-home message' – sticks in the mind long after the presentation is over.

Creating a structure

Everything in the structure of the presentation should revolve around your message.

You could use Aristotle's three modes of appeal as a structuring device (we looked at these at the start of Chapter 5):

- Start with *ethos*: establish your credentials for speaking to this audience.
- Continue with *logos*: deliver your message and a small number of supporting points (three is always a good number to aim for).
- And end with *pathos*: a rousing call to action that appeals to your audience's emotions.

If you have only a short time to plan your presentation, this three-part structure will serve you well.

MONROE'S MOTIVATED SEQUENCE

In the 1930s, Alan Monroe, a psychology professor at Purdue University in Indiana, invented a model that develops the three-part structure into a five-step sequence. Monroe suggested that, 'when confronted with a problem, people look for a solution; when they feel a want or need, they search for a way to satisfy it'. (These needs are the self-same needs that we looked at in Chapter 6.) Monroe's motivated sequence structures a presentation to exploit this desire to satisfy needs.

▶

At step one, capture the audience's attention. Ask a question, tell a story or use a quotation. Above all, say or do something *surprising*. At this point, the audience should be asking itself: 'Where is this presentation going? What's going to happen?'

At step two, convince the audience that they are confronting a problem. They may already know about this problem; showing that you understand it will increase your *ethos* with them. Or you might present them with a new, shocking problem. Create dissatisfaction and discomfort, and the need for resolution. At this point, the audience should be saying to itself: 'This is serious. What can we do?'

At step three, introduce your solution. How will it solve the problem? This is the heart of your presentation: it is where *logos* comes to the fore. Drive home your key message and lay out a small number of key points to support it. Summarize your ideas as you go, so that the audience never gets lost. At this point, they should be saying: 'This seems to be the obvious solution. But how will it work in practice? And how will it affect me?'

At step four, visualize the future. Describe how the world will look if the audience does nothing. Or describe a world in which your solution has been implemented. Or do both. At this point, the audience should be almost audibly crying out: 'Tell us what to do!'

Finally, at step five, make your call to action. Make the action simple and, if possible, immediate. And don't forget the *pathos*: we act on our emotions, so stir the audience with the emotion that is appropriate to the action you want them to take.

Monroe's motivated sequence has served presenters well for almost 90 years. It is adaptable to many different themes. Above all, it helps us to plan material that speaks directly to our audience.

Putting it on cards

The very best presenters work without notes. They speak with effortless ease, apparently improvising a seamless thread of glittering eloquence.

Don't be fooled. That spontaneity has been carefully planned and rehearsed. It represents an ideal that we could all aim for, but there is no shame in not quite achieving it. On the way to speaking without notes, you could consider writing the full text of your presentation, reading from an autocue (which displays the text you speak on a semi-transparent screen), or putting prompt notes onto cards. All three methods have advantages and challenges.

A script gives you complete control. You need never stumble over your words again! Using a script, you can choose your words carefully and you will never overrun: you can time your presentation to the second. On the other hand, you may not be very competent at reading a script; the words may remain obstinately on the page and refuse to leap into life.

An autocue releases you from the burden of looking down to read your script. You can look up and around, while actually reading your script. And that might help to energize your delivery.

Most presenters probably choose the option of notes on cards. Filing or archive cards are best; use the largest you can find. Cards have a number of key advantages:

- They are less shaky than paper – they don't rustle.
- They are more compact.
- They give your hands something firm to hold.
- They look more professional.
- They force you to write only brief notes.

By writing only brief notes, triggers and cues on your cards, you force yourself to think about what you are saying, while you are saying it. As a result, you will sound more convincing.

The challenge of using cards is that you will have to think about what to say. Those 'ums' and 'ers' may reappear; you may find yourself using irritating mannerisms or meaningless phrases (some presenters don't even notice that they are using them until they are told by a kind colleague). To overcome these glitches in delivery, try to cultivate deliberate silence while you are working out what to say.

Write your notes in bold print, using pen or felt-tip. Write on only one side and number the cards sequentially. Include:

- what you *must* say;
- what you *should* say to support the main idea;
- what you *could* say if you have time.

Keep the cards simple to look at and rehearse with them so that you get to know them. And don't forget to hold them together with a treasury tag!

PRAISE: adding spice

Exciting presentations bring ideas alive. There is a famous story about a little girl who claimed she liked plays on the radio, 'because the pictures were better'. Pictures on slides can be good; but *these* pictures – the ones you create in your audience's minds with your words – are often better.

Here are six ways in which you can stimulate your audience's imagination. We can remember them using the mnemonic PRAISE:

- *Proverbs* state ideas in memorable form. Make your message or your key points sound like advertising jingles or political slogans. Your audience will leave the presentation quoting them with delight.
- *Resonators* bring ideas to life by attaching them to vivid images. These images contain lots of sensory information: appeals to sight, sound, touch, taste, smell or feeling. They work especially

well if they involve human beings doing things. Find concrete examples that illustrate your ideas.

- *Attention-grabbers* do just that: they capture or recapture your audience's attention. Surprise and suspense work well as attention-grabbers. So do figures of speech: turns of phrase or unusual ways of using language that make ideas stand out memorably. Among the most common figures of speech are metaphor, antithesis (contrast), rhetorical questions and three-part lists.

- *Influencers* give your ideas the weight of authority. You might deliver that authority in your job title, your experience or your behaviour. Information gains authority if you point out the authority of its source or author. Presenters often try to give their ideas greater influence by quoting famous authors.

- *Stories*, as we have already seen, can be more persuasive than the most authoritative statistics. We believe stories, however fantastical: we identify with the characters and we face their challenges with them. The story of one person can often be more convincing than a mass of carefully documented evidence.

- *Emotions*, as we have already seen, influence us more strongly than reasoned argument. We act on our emotions. Colour your argument with emotion and it will touch parts of the brain that logic cannot reach.

EXERCISE

Take a Big Idea that you will be arguing for in the near future. On a piece of paper, write down some ideas for examples of each of these PRAISE techniques: proverbial expressions, resonating examples, attention-grabbers, sources of influence, stories and emotional elements.

Designing visuals

'Death by PowerPoint': it is a worryingly familiar phrase. Too many business audiences are now suffering from PowerPoint fatigue. And the overwhelming reason for this fatigue is that presenters are not using slides properly.

Put simply: presenters should be putting pictures on slides, not text.

Slides are *visual*. They should offer information that cannot be put into words. Why show a visual otherwise? This point is so blazingly obvious that it seems amazing, at first, how many presenters ignore it. But if we look at the way that slide programs have been promoted, the reason for this problem becomes clearer.

Computer slides have been sold to us as a way of making life easier for presenters. We have been told that slides make us look more prepared and – allegedly – professional. We've been told that slides can act as notes, with the audience being offered hard copy after the presentation.

We've been seduced, in other words, into putting *text* onto slides, rather than pictures.

In fact, computer-generated slides are the descendants, not of the earlier 35mm slide, but of a much older technology: the blackboard. But – unlike the blackboard – slides display text *before* the speaker speaks it, rather than *while* they speak. The audience is forced to read and listen at the same time – usually, to different text – and they do neither very well (a troubling effect that psychologists call 'cognitive dissonance'). What's more, by flashing a piece of text onto a screen in advance of talking about it, the presenter completely destroys any element of surprise or anticipation.

What's worse still, slides seduce presenters into presenting *less well*. They feel forced to 'speak to the slides' (which many do, literally), thus breaking their link with the audience. The presenter is no longer presenting: they have become a voiceover. Result: the audience loses concentration. (Think of what schoolchildren often do when their teacher turns away from them and writes on the blackboard.) Because they are not writing and speaking – as they would with a blackboard – presenters cannot decide exactly what to say: should they read out what is on the slide (which is probably too brief and vague to make sense anyway), or paraphrase it (thus increasing the cognitive dissonance for the audience)?

Of course, slides can be effective. But they should *support* your presentation, not substitute for it:

- Remove words. Unless you want to discuss a piece of text, it should not appear on a slide.

- Use pictures. Photos, maps, diagrams – any kind of graphic will do as long as it is *simple.*

- Create *visual dissonance.* An image on a slide should show *less* than the audience needs to understand it; you, the presenter, can then resolve the tension by talking about it.

If you *must* put words on slides, make them big enough for the audience to read, and put no more words on the slide than you would expect the audience to read.

Better still: turn off the projector and concentrate on presenting.

Rehearsing

Rehearsal is the reality check. I am astonished at how many presenters think they can simply turn up and run a presentation without rehearsing it. The truth is: you cannot rehearse too much. Rehearsal helps you to remember what you want to say; it helps you to get the timing right; and it helps you to master nerves.

Rehearse success. We so often rehearse failure: we imagine what will go wrong, over and over again. Instead, when you run through your presentation, imagine precisely what you will do and say – and imagine doing it brilliantly. Imagine speaking confidently and eloquently; imagine the audience listening attentively to your every word and applauding warmly when you have finished. (There is an exercise in Chapter 9 to help you rehearse success.)

Rehearse in real time; don't skip bits. Rehearse with a colleague or friend. And rehearse, if you can, at least once in the venue where you will be presenting.

Rehearsal gives you the freedom to perform when it's time to perform. Once you've rehearsed your material, you will be better prepared to concentrate on what you should be doing in the presentation itself: talking to the audience.

Controlling the audience

Your relationship with the audience matters much, much more than what you say. They will forget most of what you say. But they will remember *you*.

You are performing. Your whole body is involved. You must become aware of what your body is doing so that you can control it, and thus the audience.

Eye contact

As we said in Chapter 5, we speak more with our eyes than with our voices. Your eyes tell the audience that you are taking notice of them, that you know what you are saying and that you *believe* what you are saying.

Imagine a lighthouse beam shooting out from your eyes and scanning the audience. Make sure that the beam enters every pair of eyes in the room. Focus for a few seconds on each pair of eyes and meet their gaze.

Your face

The rest of your face is important, too! Remember to smile. Animate your face and remember to make everything just a little larger than life so that your face can be 'read' at the back of the room.

Gestures

Find the gestures that are natural for you. If you are a great gesticulator, don't try to force your hands into rigid stillness. If you don't normally gesture a great deal, don't force yourself into balletic movements. Keep your gestures open, away from your body and into the room. Don't cross your hands behind your back, and don't put them in your pockets too much. (It is a good idea to empty your pockets before the presentation so that you don't find yourself jingling coins or keys.)

Movement

Aim for stillness. This does not mean that you should stand completely still all the time. Moving about the room shows that you are making the space your own. But rhythmic, repetitive movement can be annoying and suggest the neurotic pacing of a panther in a cage. Try not to rock on your feet or tie your legs in knots! Aim to have both feet on the ground as much as possible and slow down your movements.

Looking after yourself

And you will *still* be nervous as the moment of truth approaches. Remember that those nerves are there to help you. If you have prepared adequately, you should be ready to use your nerves to encounter the uncertainty of live performance.

On some occasions, it can be useful to meet the audience and chat with them before you start. This can break the ice and put you more at ease.

Prepare your voice. Along with work on your breathing (we have already discussed 7/11 breathing earlier in this chapter), pay attention to the muscles around your mouth that help you to articulate your words. Try some tongue-twisters or sing a favourite song. Chew the cud, and get your tongue and lips really working and warmed up.

EXERCISE

A very simple exercise to bring your mouth muscles to life is to stick your tongue as far out of your mouth as you can and then speak a part of your presentation, trying to make the consonants as clear as you can. You only need to do this for about 30 seconds to wake up your voice and make it clearer. You will, of course, look rather silly while doing this, so it is best to do the exercise in a private place!

Answering questions

Many presenters are as worried about the question session as about the presentation itself. A few guidelines can help to turn your question session from a trial into a triumph:

- *Decide when to take questions.* This will probably be at the end. But you might prefer to take questions during the presentation. This is more difficult to manage but can improve your relationship with the audience.

- *Anticipate the most likely questions.* These may be 'Frequently Asked Questions' that you can easily foresee. Others may arise from the particular circumstances of the presentation.

- *Use a 'plant'.* Ask someone to be ready with a question to start off the session. Audiences are sometimes hesitant at the end of a presentation about breaking the atmosphere.

- *Answer concisely.* Force yourself to be brief.

- *Answer honestly.* You can withhold information, but don't lie. Someone in the audience will almost certainly see through you.

- *Take questions from the whole audience.* From all parts of the room and from different 'social areas'.

- *Answer the whole audience.* Don't let questions seduce you into private conversations. Make sure the audience has heard the question.

- *If you don't know, say so.* And promise what you will do later to answer the question.

SUMMARY POINTS

- To make an effective presentation means taking control of:
  - the material;
  - the audience;
  - yourself.
- To prepare the material:
  - define your objective;
  - analyse your audience;
  - construct a message;
  - create a structure (Monroe's motivated sequence); ▶

- put it on cards;
- add spice (PRAISE);
- design visuals;
- rehearse.
- To control the audience, work on:
  - eye contact;
  - facial expression;
  - gestures;
  - movement.
- To look after yourself, pay attention to:
  - breathing;
  - articulation;
  - a strategy of answering questions.

8 Putting it in writing

Writing well is challenging. It takes skill, creativity and a certain level of technical knowledge. But perhaps the greatest challenge is that our writing has to communicate without us.

Think back to our key communication question. *What effect am I having?* In a conversation, answering that question may be hard; but it is a whole lot harder if we are writing to someone. Our reader is judging us in our absence. The tone of our writing suggests the kind of person we are; and the reader may read a tone in our writing that we did not intend. Added to that, in normal conversation our listener is unlikely to think much about any mistakes we make when we speak (we discussed this in Chapter 2); but in our writing, they may well notice errors of grammar, spelling or punctuation. And they will judge us – at least in part – by those errors.

Writing itself is changing fast. We read less on paper and more on screen. Formal reports are becoming increasingly complemented by relatively informal e-mails and the immediacy of texting, messaging and tweeting. And behind all these developments lies another trend, almost unnoticed – until we pick up a pen.

Most of the time, we are not actually writing – we're *printing*. In the workplace, very few of us now see anyone's handwriting. Printing creates another barrier between us and our readers. Paradoxically, at just the time when social media encourages us to think of writing as a form of conversation, printing makes our writing less personal. All these developments are changing the way we read, which means that we have to think even more carefully about how to write well.

Let's start by considering the most common form of writing in the workplace.

The trouble with e-mail

In the time that it takes you to read this sentence, 20 million e-mails have been written. We apparently spend over 11 hours a week reading and answering our e-mails at work. And we read at least 30 per cent of them on mobile devices.

It is hardly any wonder that so many e-mails are misunderstood. We could blame carelessness, or the sense of urgency that makes us write e-mails too quickly. But the medium itself also contributes to the problem. E-mail lacks what the psychologists call para-linguistic information: the information we glean from a speaker's facial expressions, gestures and tone of voice.

We assume that e-mail is like a conversation. So we assume that we are using these non-verbal elements when we write – and that our reader can see and hear them. Professor Justin Kruger of New York University, and his colleagues, found that these assumptions have three consistent effects:

- First, we are significantly less clear in our e-mails than we are in real conversations.
- Second, we generally overestimate how clear our e-mails are.
- And third, we consistently overestimate how well we understand the e-mails we read.

Professor Kruger found that these misjudgements were especially serious when e-mail writers tried to convey double meanings: irony, for example, or sarcasm.

Research by Professor Kristin Byron of Syracuse University takes these findings further. She found that we tend to read e-mails as more emotionally negative than the writer intended. We are likely to interpret intended positive expressions as emotionally neutral, and neutral expressions as more emotionally negative. For example, a writer may think that they are making a simple comment, but the reader may interpret that comment as criticism. According to Professor Byron, we are even more likely to interpret e-mails negatively if we perceive the writer to be higher in status than us, older, or – interestingly – male.

What is going on here? I think that, in assuming unconsciously that we are engaged in conversation, the text of the e-mail – and, even more, the screen on which we read it – acts like a mask. Talking to someone wearing a mask feels intimidating; e-mail, perhaps, generates a similar unconscious feeling of threat.

Avoiding misunderstandings

Four strategies may help us to reduce the possibility of misunderstanding. They all rely on making ourselves more visible to the reader, somehow, in our e-mails.

First, we could use 'display rules'. For example, senders increasingly add disclaimers to e-mails such as: 'Please excuse the shortness of this e-mail, it is sent from my iPad.' In one organization, all e-mails apparently end with the words: 'This e-mail may display a telegraphic style that gives the false impression of curtness or insensitivity.'

Second, we could use emotional cues. If we explain explicitly how we are feeling, our reader will be less likely to misinterpret what we write. Use phrases like 'this situation makes me feel...' or 'actually, right now, I feel... about this.' Emoticons also act as emotional cues; recent research suggests that we now read the symbol :-) with the part of the brain that interprets real facial expressions. However, some readers may see emoticons as less authentic than other emotional cues, such as how long we take to answer an e-mail, how long our message is, or how formally we express ourselves.

Third, we could use e-mail etiquette. This is really no more than a version of the politeness that we use in real conversations; it simply requires a little more effort when we are writing:

- Avoid the elements that readers are most likely to misunderstand: ambiguity, irony, sarcasm, humour. You know how easily a humorous remark can go wrong in conversation – think how much more likely it is to create a problem when it is written down.

- Add in some kindness, thoughtfulness and good manners. At the very least, use salutations, sign-offs and 'handshakes': those little relationship-building remarks at the beginning and end of an e-mail.

- Avoid CAPITAL LETTERS; they look as if you are shouting. Avoid underlining: it makes text harder to read. And avoid excessive use of italics or exclamation marks, which can make your e-mail look too excitable.

Finally, we could pay attention to the one element that e-mail often lacks: context. If the reader cannot work out what this e-mail is about, they will remain baffled. They cannot ask you (unless they send yet another e-mail); we need to help them. Include some framing information: past history, recent activity, the last conversation you held. Setting the scene may seem like waffling to you, but it will help your reader to tune in more quickly to what you are saying.

Building credit with your reader

Misunderstandings often arise when we e-mail someone to ask them to do something. A simple request can be misinterpreted as a curt order; an instruction to change something can be read as criticism. How can we use e-mail to persuade people to act, without causing offence?

Think of your relationship with your reader as being like a bank account. If you want to draw on that account, you will probably need to put some funds in first. How can you add credit to your relationship with the reader? What can you offer them? Simply telling someone to do something can easily be interpreted as 'pushing' them; if you can find a way to 'pull' them towards the action you are seeking, you may get a more positive response. Thanking, praising, encouraging and helping all count as deposits in the bank account of your working relationship.

Try to think – and write – collaboratively. Mirroring can work well: using the reader's language suggests that you are thinking like them. But aligning can work even better: find the common cause, contribute something to it and *then* ask for help.

The writer Jay Heinrichs suggests thinking also about the tense you use in your e-mails. We use three tenses: past, present and future. Each carries hidden meanings, especially if we are asking our reader to do something:

- We associate the *past tense*, unconsciously, with blame or self-justification. Did this happen? Should it have happened? Who was responsible? Who should be punished?
- The *present tense* deals in values. It implicitly tells the reader what kind of person you are, and what values you hold.
- The *future tense* is about choice. It suggests decision making. The future tense leaps past blame and values, and seeks to do the right thing.

The tense to avoid, if possible, is the past. It can suggest blame, and it locks us into the past. You are looking for action *in the future*. Focus on the present tense to bond with your reader, and on the future tense to create solutions.

From speaking to writing

E-mail is just one example of a general trend. The distinction between writing and speaking is becoming increasingly blurred. A formal style of writing increasingly sounds impersonal and distant; more and more, we are demanding written language that 'sounds' more like speech. Hence the calls for plain English, for example, and the regular lampooning of 'gobbledegook' in the newspapers.

But reading is not like listening in a conversation. It takes more effort (and, of course, a certain level of education that listening does not require). It is worth remembering that most of our readers – at work, at least – probably don't *want* to read what we have written. They are usually reading only because they *must* do so.

So our task as writers is to make reading as easy as possible.

The reader contract

Your reader is making a contract with you. They are willing to give your writing a certain level of attention for a certain length of time. A reader scrolling through their e-mails on their mobile device is not strongly committed to reading; their attention span is short, and your e-mail is battling against a host of other information and distractions. A reader of a lengthy report, in contrast, will only begin to read if they are relatively committed to reading it; they are willing to give you more attention in the hope of a more substantial return. The reader contract, then, is somewhere on this spectrum between committed and uncommitted.

You need to respond to that contract. At the uncommitted end of the spectrum, your e-mail must deliver your message as quickly as possible, and you must offer only information that is directly relevant to your reader and your purpose. In your report, by contrast, you can take more time; you can offer information that is more objective and more detailed.

The style spectrum

The style spectrum responds to the reader contract. With uncommitted readers, your style needs to be immediate, simple, direct – closer, perhaps, to spoken language. With committed readers, your style can be more measured, less personal and more formal. More like writing, in fact.

Different kinds of writing tend to sit at different places on the style spectrum. E-mail sits at the informal end, along with leaflets, brochures, information sheets, magazine articles, blog posts and web pages. Reports sit at the formal end of the style spectrum, with minutes of meetings, proposals, research papers and academic essays.

However formal our style, we must always aim to be readable. Writing that is too informal will collapse into incoherence: sentences will ramble or remain incomplete; the writer might use idioms or slang that the reader finds incomprehensible or unacceptable. Very formal writing might include long, unfamiliar words and complicated sentences. It will convey no personality or warmth; it will be dry as dust.

We can choose where to place our writing on the formality spectrum. Neither end of the spectrum is in any way superior to the other. The trick is to pick the style that works for our reader – and for the type of document we're writing.

Writing as you speak

People often tell me: 'I'm not a good writer. I write as I speak.' In fact, writing as you speak is perhaps one of the best ways to become a better writer.

The best way to write as you speak is to imagine speaking to your reader, and write down *exactly* what you would say to them. Doing this brings a number of benefits:

- You will naturally adapt your style to the reader you are speaking to.
- You will create more text than you need, which gives you plenty to edit.
- You will tend to get the grammar and punctuation right.

That last point sometimes surprises people. But in truth, most of us speak grammatically most of the time. And punctuation began as a set of marks indicating how to speak written words. So writing as you speak is a good first step towards a good piece of writing.

But it's not the last step.

Editing your work

Editing helps our writing to communicate without us: without the help of all that paralinguistic information in our voice, face and gestures. As well as making our draft clearer, editing also helps us to correct any errors. The aim of editing is to make reading as easy as possible.

Editing adapts our style on three levels. We can look at the words we use, the sentences we write and the paragraphs we construct.

Choosing words wisely

Four features mark out our words as formal or informal. We can think about:

- long words and short words;
- passive verbs and active verbs;
- abstract nouns;
- unnecessary words.

We can adjust each feature to adjust the style of our writing.

LONG WORDS OR SHORT WORDS?

English has a huge vocabulary. It has grown out of many other languages: French, Latin and a host of languages from northern Europe. As a result, English often has two or three words meaning roughly (or *approximately*) the same thing. We can *try* or *endeavour*; we can *start*, *begin* or *commence* doing something; we can *anticipate* or *foresee*.

Which are the best words to choose? It depends where you want your writing to sit on the style spectrum. For historical reasons, long words in English are more formal than short ones. *I anticipate that the project will conclude successfully* is more formally expressed than *I expect the project to succeed*.

Many authorities on writing, especially those advocating plain English, tell us to choose short words rather than longer ones. This makes some sense: more people understand the word *chew* than the word *ruminate*, for example. But sometimes the longer word has a more exact meaning: *rumination*, in this example, is a particular *kind* of chewing. The long word may work better for us sometimes than the shorter one: in technical writing, or if we are writing to a reader whose first language is not English. *Prefer* the short word to the long word; but don't assume that the shorter word is better.

PASSIVE VERBS OR ACTIVE VERBS?

Verbs can be either active or passive. An active verb expresses what its subject does; a passive verb expresses what its subject suffers.

> *The report **was written** by Sola.*
> *Sola **wrote** the report.*

Sentences with passive verbs make your writing more formal, and active verbs more informal. In general, prefer active verbs to passive ones; but don't rule out passive verbs. They can help you to structure a sentence to emphasize a point differently; they can be useful when you don't know – or don't want to say – who did something. Passive verbs are not wrong; but active verbs bring your writing to life.

WHAT DO YOU MEAN, 'ABSTRACT NOUNS'?

Nouns name things, people, times, places or qualities. *Concrete nouns* name things physically present in the world (*table, woman, pen, car, tree*); *abstract nouns* name ideas, concepts or qualities that cannot be sensed physically (*growth, awareness, training, marketing, possibility*).

Abstract nouns make your writing more formal. Many abstract nouns are longer words with standard endings: *-ion* (*translation, manipulation, specification*); *-ment* (*measurement, management, replacement*); *-ence* or *-ance* (*governance, maintenance, predominance*); or *-ity* (*acidity, functionality, superiority*).

To make your writing more formal, pile on the abstract nouns. If you want to make your writing less formal, replace abstract nouns with verbs or adjectives. If the only way to replace an abstract noun is to use a group of words, consider keeping it.

WHICH WORDS DO I NEED?

Some words contribute little to your meaning, but a lot to your tone. *We do these tests every week* says the same thing as *We perform these tests on a weekly basis*, but the second version undoubtedly sounds more professional and impressive. Using words – and adding words – to impress will make your writing more formal. If you remove them, your writing will 'sound' more direct, more 'spoken' – but also, perhaps, less polite. Generally, your writing will improve if it says more with fewer words:

> *The benefits of this arrangement are a saving in consultancy costs and the opportunity for new users to learn the system in*

a meaningful situation at the same time as they learn their jobs.

This arrangement saves consultancy costs and allows new users to learn the system as part of on-the-job learning.

EXERCISE

Pick an e-mail that you wrote some time ago. Rewrite it, choosing to shift its style towards one or other end of the style spectrum. Try to say exactly the same thing as in the original; try not to alter the meaning. What do you notice about the rewrites? How do you think the reader would react to your new version?

Constructing stunning sentences

Sentences express ideas. They will express your ideas more strongly if you construct them well. Longer, more complicated sentences sound more formal; shorter, simpler sentences sound more informal. But this is not an iron rule: extremely informal writing might include very long, rambling sentences. Aim always to write as *clearly* as possible, however formal your style.

Follow the '15–25' rule. Message sentences, topic sentences and other sentences expressing big ideas should never exceed 15 words. All other sentences should be no more than 25 words long.

Strengthen sentences by:

- cutting up long sentences into shorter, separate sentences;
- simplifying complicated sentences;
- finding strong subjects and verbs.

Put the subject as close to the start of the sentence as you can, and follow it as closely as possible with its verb. Try to choose subjects that act like characters in a story, and use the verb to say what the character is doing in the story. This sentence, for example, contains no characters: *The decision will be made on Friday*. The effect is very formal and distant. *The board will make its decision on Friday* introduces a character and the sense of a story. Of course, we could make the style of this sentence even more informal by removing the abstract noun: *The board will decide on Friday*.

Creating powerful paragraphs

Paragraphs indicate a certain level of formality in your writing. Reports, briefing papers and proposals always benefit from good paragraphing. E-mails, in contrast, use paragraphs only sparingly. And the most informal writing – advertising, campaigning material, speeches – tend to be written more in single sentences than in paragraphs.

Paragraphs display the shape of your thinking. They show the individual main ideas and the relationships between them. Every time you make a new point, start a new paragraph.

Use a topic sentence at the start of each paragraph to summarize it. Topic sentences help you to decide what to include in each paragraph. You can think of a topic sentence as the paragraph's message. It should:

- be a fully grammatical sentence;
- make a single point;
- contain no more than 15 words;
- say something new.

Where can you find good topic sentences? You could write your paragraph first, then find the sentence that summarizes it. You could ask what you want to say in the paragraph, write down your topic sentence, and then construct your paragraph to support it. Often, you can find a topic sentence by looking at a paragraph's *last* sentence. Flip that concluding point to the top of the paragraph and see how well it works as a topic sentence.

EDITING A PARAGRAPH

To minimize potential downtime and operational risk, it is recommended that the business case for the purchase of a back-up server, which could also be used for system testing, be formally examined. We are now addressing this since a decision is needed by the end of March to avoid additional hire costs or the loss of the rented machine.

Note how a topic sentence helps us to shorten this paragraph and make it more readable:

We are now examining the business case for buying a back-up server. This could:

- *minimize potential downtime;*
- *minimize operational risk;*
- *also be used for system testing.*

A decision is needed by the end of March to avoid extra hire costs or the loss of the rented machine.

Putting it all together: a strategy for editing

Editing helps us to say what we want to say more clearly. Whether we are aiming for a formal, more 'written' style, or a more informal style that is closer to speaking, we need to polish our writing so that it works as well as possible without all the gestures, facial expressions and vocal inflections that we bring to our conversations.

The most efficient strategy is to edit on these three levels, *in this order*:

- paragraphs;
- sentences;
- words.

Editing paragraphs will solve many problems at the sentence and word level, almost without our having to worry about them. And improving our sentence construction will automatically mean changing the words we use.

Add these top tips to make your editing strategy even more effective:

- Print it out. Your text looks different on paper: more immediate, less glassy. And it is sitting in your *hand*. You will spot more errors than if you are staring at a screen.
- Take a break. Even if you are facing a tight deadline, walk away from your draft and come back to edit it. Even 30 seconds makes a difference. The longer the break, the better.
- Read it out loud. The best writing sounds elegant and eloquent. It makes its point with no fuss. Listen for the places where your writing jangles and grates.
- Pretend you are the intended audience. Is it possible that they will misinterpret what you have said, or – more importantly – the way you've said it? Check out ambiguous expressions, humour and complicated expressions.
- Use the readability statistics. You will find them on your computer, if you're using Word. Look under the 'Review' tab at the 'Spelling and Grammar' dialogue boxes (or look up 'readability statistics' on your search engine.) These statistics are not subtle, but they do give you an objective measure of readability. And they can confirm that you are editing in the right direction.

- Be ruthless. The final step is to cut out whatever you don't need. Chop out words, sentences – even whole paragraphs, if you can. What remains will sparkle like a diamond.

SUMMARY POINTS

- Most of our writing in the workplace is likely to be e-mail.
- We assume that e-mail is like a conversation. As a result:
  - We are significantly less clear in our e-mails than we are in real conversations.
  - We generally overestimate how clear our e-mails are.
  - We consistently overestimate how well we understand the e-mails we read.
  - We tend to read e-mails as more emotionally negative than the writer intended.
- Four strategies may help us to reduce the possibility of misunderstanding:
  - Use 'display rules'.
  - Use emotional cues.
  - Use e-mail etiquette.
  - Add contextual material to our e-mails.
- Think of your relationship with your reader as being like a bank account. How can you add credit to your relationship with the reader?
- Mirror your reader's language and align with them in finding a common cause.
- Your reader is making a contract with you. They are either committed or uncommitted to reading.

▶

- The style of your writing should respond to that level of commitment. For a committed reader, your style can be more formal. For an uncommitted reader, make your style less formal and more 'spoken'.
- Imagine speaking to your reader, and write down *exactly* what you would say to them.
- Edit your work on three levels: paragraphs, sentences, words.
- Edit paragraphs by using topic sentences.
- Edit sentences by:
  - cutting up long sentences into shorter, separate sentences;
  - simplifying complicated sentences;
  - finding strong subjects and verbs.
- Edit words by:
  - preferring short words to long words;
  - preferring active verbs to passive verbs;
  - removing abstract nouns;
  - cutting unnecessary words.
- Adopt a strategy for editing:
  - Print it out.
  - Take a break.
  - Read it out loud.
  - Pretend you are the intended audience.
  - Use the readability statistics.
  - Be ruthless.

9 Networking: the new conversation

Networking is a new name for an old idea. A survey by Common Purpose in 2008 found that 68 per cent of business leaders expected their networking activity to increase over the next five years. Among younger business leaders, the number rose to 75 per cent.

First things first. Networking is *not*:

- selling;
- using other people for your own gain;
- putting people on the spot.

Effective networkers understand that we need other people to fulfil our ambitions and dreams. Networking is a tool to help us find those people.

Networking can be strategic or spontaneous. At its best, strategic networking prepares us for the spontaneous moments of discovery.

To network or not to network?

According to the *Oxford English Dictionary*, the word 'network' – meaning an interconnected group of people – first appeared in 1946. The words 'networker' and 'networking', referring to the activities of such groups, do not appear in print until 1976.

Networking has, from the start, been associated with the rise of the businesswoman. In 1980, Mary-Scott Welch published *Networking: The great new way for women to get ahead*. According to her obituary in the *New York Times*, the book was written 'in an era when more women were competing for jobs traditionally dominated by men'. *Networking* also included the first recorded use of the word 'network' as a verb: 'this book', wrote Ms Welch, 'will show you how to network'.

Networking thus arguably offers a way of doing business that is less aggressively masculine. Networking emphasizes cooperation and collaboration, rather than individualism and competitiveness.

What makes networking effective?

Effective networking relies on three key qualities:

- an 'abundance mentality';
- generosity;
- reciprocity.

CULTIVATING AN 'ABUNDANCE MENTALITY'

People with a 'scarcity mentality' have difficulty sharing. They feel that success depends on holding on to their resources – property, knowledge, relationships. For them, victory means someone else's defeat, and everyone is out for themselves.

People with an 'abundance mentality', in contrast, understand that human resources – knowledge, intelligence, imagination – produce more when they are shared. For them, victory only occurs when we all win; everyone has something unique to offer. An abundance mentality suggests that there are always three ways to do anything: your way, my way – and a better way.

BEING GENEROUS

With an abundance mentality, we can give attention to others; and, as we have seen in Chapter 4, attention is at the heart of effective listening. We can also give information more easily and less egotistically.

FOSTERING RECIPROCITY

None of us can survive without the help of others. Humans seem to be 'hard-wired' for reciprocity; if I give you something, you will almost certainly feel obliged to offer me something in return. (Reciprocity is one of Robert Cialdini's patterns of influence, which we explored in Chapter 5.) Collaboration requires trust; and reciprocity provides the currency of trust.

Preparing to network

As with any other communication skill, strategic networking benefits from careful preparation. Having a plan will help you to network more effectively and monitor your success afterwards.

Preparing yourself

Networking puts us on the spot. However politely we skirt around the subject, the first thing we want to know about someone is who they are: not just a name, but an identity. We are looking for something we can relate to, something we can recognize and feel comfortable with. It helps to have a clear 'script' that we can draw on to present ourselves clearly and easily to others.

Build your brand

Our brand is what others know us to be. It is not our personality, or our mission in life. It is closer to *ethos*, but more immediate. Our brand sends the message we want others to know about us.

Think of your brand as sitting 'on the surface'. Other qualities sit below the surface: your beliefs, values, attitudes. Your brand suggests those values.

EXERCISE

Spend a little time working out a few of your core values:

- What matters to you?
- If you didn't have to work, what would you do?
- What puts you 'in the zone'?
- What big problems would you like to do something about?
- What would you like people to say about you at your 75th birthday party?
- Who are your heroes?
- What makes you proud about yourself?
- What makes you different from everyone else?

We demonstrate our values in our achievements. Our achievements are instant talking points; they provide evidence of experience and expertise that others might be looking for.

It is not always easy to remember everything we have achieved. If you make a list of your accomplishments, they will be ready in the background for you to use.

EXERCISE

This exercise has a double benefit. It will help you to prepare to network; and it will help you to update your CV.

Make a note of what you are good at, experienced with, trained in and successful at. Note down also how those skills have helped you in specific projects, sports activities, educational or training courses, or work in the community.

Keep the skills and the activities separate. For each skill, look for further examples of activities. For each activity, ask what other skills it demonstrates.

It is up to you to acknowledge and celebrate your accomplishments. And when you start to talk about what you have achieved, you will begin to speak with passion about something you care about: always an infectious pleasure in conversation.

Create a self-introduction

We introduce ourselves to others so often that it is worth thinking about how to do it well. A self-introduction that develops rapport and generates interest can be one of our greatest networking assets.

Develop a self-introduction that you feel comfortable with. Practise different forms of words and see which ones trigger interest and intrigue.

YOUR SELF-INTRODUCTION: A CHECKLIST

Keep it short	Find the headline that summarizes what you do in a single sentence.
Use a verb	State what you do – not what you are. Your introduction will be more dynamic and less ambiguous. 'I specialize in minor injuries at an A&E unit' is much more interesting than 'I'm a nurse'.
Be distinctive	What marks you out from others? What is different about what you do? What's the thing you really like doing?
Provide hooks	Use familiar language, not jargon or technical terms. Above all, keep using verbs: those 'doing' words will bring you alive in the other person's mind.
Engage	Beware the temptation to apologize for your existence! Smile; use clear and steady eye contact; avoid words like 'just' and 'only' ('I'm just a secretary'; 'I'm only here because my manager asked me to come').

Many of us find it uncomfortable to 'blow our own trumpet'. But we don't need to play loudly or boisterously! People need to know what you have to offer, so that they can call on your talents. You know what you have to offer, and how good it is. You need to make it *visible*.

Marshal your resources

As with any other kind of communication, we have resources in three major areas that can help us. They are the resources that help us to build the rapport we explored back in Chapter 1. *Visual* resources include how we look and behave; our *vocal* resources are our voice and the parts of our body that support voice production; and *verbal* resources are the words we use.

Visual resources

Looks matter. Looking good shows that you respect the people you are meeting:

- *Think about your wardrobe.* Build a clothes collection that represents your own values elegantly and simply. Buy a few, good-quality outfits that you can mix and match. Darker colours generally work better than lighter shades: they hide stains and flatter the figure more effectively; and they tend to give an air of authority. If in doubt, dress *up* for the occasion – it is easier to adjust on the spot than if we are underdressed.

- *Use accessories wisely.* Learn how the extras can pull your image together. Jewellery, ties, scarves, bags, cases – they may project your brand more powerfully than your clothes. Coordination is key.

- *Pay attention to grooming.* The state of your shoes, nails and hair matter. You are meeting people close up. It is worth thinking even about your breath.

- *Mind your manners.* How you stand, move and make eye contact all say something about you. Pay attention to posture. The best thing you can wear is a smile.

Vocal resources

The quality of your voice also matters. Volume, pace and pitch are the three core elements of our voice; we instinctively read a great deal about a person from our perceptions of these three vocal dimensions:

- *Make yourself heard.* You will probably be speaking against a babble of other voices. Direct your voice clearly at the other person; if they look as if they are straining to hear you, help by raising the volume a little.
- *Slow down.* Articulate clearly and don't gabble. Rushing your words suggests nervousness or lack of interest. Use the breathing techniques mentioned in Chapter 6.
- *Lower your tone.* A thin, high-pitched voice will suggest a lack of authority or confidence. Use the 7/11 exercise from Chapter 7.
- *Use your own accent.* Be proud of your voice: it is a vital component of your identity. If your accent is distinct or strong, people may have to work a little harder to adjust to your voice.
- *Speak clearly.* Make sure all the consonants are clear when you speak (all the letters that are not *A*, *E*, *I*, *O* or *U*). Use your lips and tongue well.

Verbal resources

Among your verbal resources are your self-introduction and the rapport-building remarks and questions. Listen, also, for the words the other person uses and adjust your vocabulary to theirs. Echoing the actual words a person uses can help to build rapport very quickly, if done subtly.

Do you have a card?

Your business card is the trace you leave behind you. It represents you in someone's memory after you have finished talking. If they want to meet you again, they use your card to do so:

- *The card should reflect your 'brand'.* Does the design say what you want it to say? Do the colours and typefaces suggest your values and style? Are they compatible with your website or blog, if you have one?
- *Essential information should be easy to see.* Your name, your company and the contact details should leap off the card.
- *Make use of space.* Don't clutter the card with unnecessary pictures or design features.
- *Quality pays.* Choose durable, good-quality card. It is almost certainly worth having your card printed professionally, if you can afford it.

If you are new to the job market, or between jobs, take the trouble to create a new card containing your contact details. Handing out a card with outdated information is not a good idea – and makes an even worse impression if the information is hastily crossed out or overwritten. You may feel uncomfortable offering a stranger your address; a telephone number and e-mail address is quite sufficient.

Look after your inner self

Networking is exhausting. Most of us meet a few new people every day, but few of us find it natural meeting dozens of new people in a couple of hours. Every new meeting is an opportunity, but it is also a challenge.

Building up your confidence

Take care not to rehearse failure. (Remember the notes on rehearsing in Chapter 7.) Instead of playing out all the scenarios that could go wrong, rehearse yourself succeeding at the networking event.

Rehearsing success is not 'positive thinking'; it is running successful conversations in our heads, in a carefully disciplined way.

EXERCISE

Here's how to rehearse success:

1 Make yourself comfortable, in a quiet room, and close your eyes. Remove all distractions.

2 Imagine a television set. Set it down across the room and switch it on.

3 On the television screen, run a video of yourself performing well at a networking meeting. Watch the video carefully and notice what 'you' are doing. Now adjust the video to make it really compelling. Turn up the sound; increase the screen size. Now, step into the movie so that you are seeing the action through your own eyes, as if you were already there. Become aware of what you are *doing*, how you *look*, how you *sound* and how you *feel*.

4 Now step out again and shift your viewpoint a little way into the future beyond the event. Now you are looking back on it, taking notes and thinking about what you did well. Notice how you feel about it now.

5 Come back to now. Freeze-frame the video at a point where you can easily remember the image. That image will be your access point into the video, so that you can rerun it whenever you want.

Identifying goals

Now that you have prepared yourself, you need to set yourself clear goals for the networking event.

It is useful to think of your goals in terms of what you want, and what you want to give. How will you know that you have got what you want? Or that you have given what you intend to give?

Sometimes we are set goals or targets by our managers. If so, make sure you are happy with what you're being asked to achieve; negotiate if necessary, so that you feel in control of your goals.

The skills of networking conversations

However much you prepare, the moment comes when you have to walk into the room and start talking to someone.

There is no one way of doing this. Some people cannot resist starting with a humorous remark; others use well-established lines like: 'Have we met before?' or 'What brings you here?' The important thing is to do it. Make contact.

Establishing rapport

Look back at the exercise on building rapport in Chapter 1. That five-step strategy is guaranteed to help you network. Start positive or neutral. Avoid emotive subjects such as religion and politics – at least to start with – and be very careful about assumptions linking one person with another. 'Are you two married?' can be an embarrassing opener – as I found to my cost a few nights before writing this chapter.

It is more than likely that you will not remember the person's name within the first few minutes of your conversation. Too much else will be going on. A few simple tricks will help a name to stick:

- *Use their name* on first introductions:
  - *Hi, I'm Megan.*
  - *Megan, hi. Pleased to meet you. I'm Tony.*
- *Ask for the name again if necessary.* Taking the trouble to ask is another gift that will be appreciated.
- *Use the other person's name once or twice during the conversation.* Some people tend to be better at doing this than others. It might feel a little awkward or false, but it will help you to remember the name.

Keeping the conversation going

In the early stages of a conversation, try to listen more than speaking. Be the first to ask a question; then listen to the answer. Make sure that it is an open question, beginning with one of the six 'w's:

- *What do you do for a living?*
- *Where do you meet most of your clients?*
- *When did you start on this line of business?*
- *Who is your link with the host organization?*
- *How did you start out?*
- *Why did you take this path?*

Now share something about yourself. (Remember the rule in that exercise in Chapter 1: no more than three questions before you make a different kind of move.) Try to link your remark to what the other person has said. Summarize and paraphrase. Check your understanding of what the other person is saying; this keeps you focused, gives you time to think of something else to say and shows that you are listening.

Another way to keep the conversation going is to bring someone else in:

Chris, come and join us. We're just talking about...
I know who you should meet. Let me try to find Firoze...

'Passing the ball' in this way can relax or enhance a conversation. It can also be a good way to bring a conversation to a close politely: having introduced people to each other, you can excuse yourself and move on.

Joining groups

Approaching a group of people differs slightly from approaching an individual. Being able to 'read' the group is helpful:

- *Arrive early.* One of the best ways to manage groups is to be in at the start of one.
- *Use previous contacts.* Everyone you speak to early in the event is a potential 'joiner' later: use one as a link person if you want to join a group.
- *Judge the tightness of the group.* How closely are people standing to each other? How is their eye contact? Can you see an opening, or is the group broadcasting its exclusivity by turning all backs on the rest of the room?
- *Exploit fractures.* Conversations rarely survive being extended beyond three people. Groups of four or more will probably be audiences, listening to a single, dominant person. You could join the audience; or you could look for two people talking and gently insinuate yourself as a third.
- *Pick off stragglers.* Not everyone in the group will be entirely 'in the circle'. Find someone at the edge – perhaps they are looking as if they want an excuse to move on – and approach them.
- *Use listening time to establish your presence.* Make eye contact; respond to what someone says with smiles and nods. Ask them a question.
- *Ask permission.* Find different ways of asking permission to enter new space:
  - *Excuse me, I don't mean to interrupt, but I overheard you talking about...*

152   **Improve Your Communication Skills**

> – *Forgive me for interrupting,* but am I right in thinking that...?
> – *Sorry to barge in, but can I just ask you about what you were saying?*

'Playing host' is a brilliant way to break into groups. Pick up a bottle of wine or a plate of nibbles and circulate. You are putting people at their ease; you're offering gifts (always a great way to get people interested in you); you're able to introduce people to each other. Playing host also helps *you*: it gives you a certain authority (or at least something to do), and it gives you control. You can judge when to stay with someone and when to move on.

Closing the conversation

Whether the conversation has gone well, or not gone anywhere in particular, take care to close it well. The final impression we make is almost as important as the first one.

Never leave someone abruptly. To exit a conversation simply, find a way to connect the person to someone else. Make the introduction; make sure that it has stuck (are they actually exchanging more than one remark with each other?); and walk away. Alternatively, use a plausible reason for leaving. Maybe you are expecting a colleague to arrive; maybe there is someone you need to speak to before they leave.

The parting stage of a conversation should always involve action of some sort. Lots of actions could end a conversation. You could:

- invite the person to meet someone else;
- make a gift of information (or food, or drink...);
- agree to meet again;
- exchange cards.

Exchanging cards

The etiquette of exchanging business cards has become more sophisticated in recent years. Business cards are gifts; treat them as such and you will not go far wrong:

- *Keep your cards in good condition.* This applies to cards you receive as well as your own. Business cardholders are a good idea; one for your own, one for cards offered.
- *Give your card respectfully.* Choose who you offer your card to. Give your card when it is asked for; asking for a card is a compliment, so treat it as such. Ask permission to offer your card. If you give your card with respect, you will instil respect for yourself. Above all, don't leave a pile of cards on a table.
- *Receive cards with respect.* The person offering is also paying a compliment, by trusting you with their contact details. Treat the card as a gift. Take it carefully; look at it; read it (aloud, perhaps); offer a compliment or a positive comment ('What an interesting design'; 'Ah, I see you're based in London'). Put the card away respectfully, perhaps only after you have parted.

It is a good idea to make notes on business cards: where you met, who introduced you, interesting information, agreed follow-up actions. However, you should never write on a business card in the other person's presence. (Unless they give you permission to do so, of course.)

Following up and building your network

Don't waste the opportunities you have worked so hard for. Once you have made contact with people, think about how you can make use of that contact. Review your cards and notes at the end of the event. Record in your diary any obvious or immediate plans for follow-up.

Find a way of organizing your network contacts. If you can align your system to other systems you use for personal details – your personal organizer, your e-mail archives – so much the better.

Reconnecting with people

Having the contacts is of little use if you don't use them. There are lots of ways of reconnecting to people you have met. You could follow up fast, send a gift – information, links to resources or other people – or invite them to make contact. Don't annoy or exhaust your new contacts, but gentle 'nudges' over time might work. A good way to maintain contact is to ask for help.

The Netbank

We have a 'net account' with everyone in our network. Just like a real bank account, our net accounts with people can be in credit or overdrawn. (Whenever we say 'I'm in your debt', or 'I'm obliged', we are signalling the need to balance our net account with someone.)

Diane Darling suggests that the best way to check our net balance with someone is to try to make a withdrawal:

- When you need to call them, will you feel comfortable doing so?
- How long has it been since you put something into the account?
- The last time they asked you to help, did you do so?

If you think your net account with someone is dangerously low, make a deposit:

- Find something you can do for the person.
- Don't ask them for anything.
- Identify people with whom you are in 'net credit'. Could they help you with a 'net loan'?

Deposits in your Netbank gather 'net interest'. A small deposit can quickly garner bigger returns.

Exploring

Effective networkers go sideways! They use every opportunity to practise their networking skills and actively look for new business relationships.

Find new ways of making your voice heard. The technologies of networking are growing fast: social networking sites, e-mail, instant messaging, blogging... Explore how you can use electronic media to promote your messages and offer useful gifts to people in your network.

THE 10 COMMANDMENTS OF EFFECTIVE NETWORKING

1 You get what you give.
2 Be yourself.
3 Honour your relationships.
4 Share; don't hoard.
5 Ask for what you want.
6 Promote yourself professionally.
7 Move on when necessary.
8 Record all your contacts.
9 Follow up.
10 Expand your horizons.

SUMMARY POINTS

- Networking is the art of building and sustaining mutually beneficial relationships.
- Networking is *not*:
  - selling;
  - using other people for your own gain;
  - putting people on the spot.
- What makes networking effective:
  - an abundance mentality;
  - generosity;
  - reciprocity.
- Prepare to network by:
  - preparing yourself;
  - building your brand;
  - finding your core values;
  - listing your achievements and accomplishments;
  - creating a self-introduction;
  - marshalling your resources: visual, vocal, verbal.
- Your business card should:
  - reflect your brand;
  - be easy to read;
  - be of high quality.
- Look after your inner self:
  - build up your confidence;
  - rehearse success;
  - identify your goals.

- In the networking conversation:
  - establish rapport;
  - use techniques to keep the conversation going;
  - practise joining groups;
  - close the conversation respectfully;
  - use good etiquette for exchanging cards.
- To follow up and build your network:
  - record your contacts;
  - reconnect with people;
  - ask for help;
  - create a network map;
  - keep the connections alive;
  - volunteer;
  - use your organization's facilities;
  - start your own network;
  - explore;
  - find new ways of making your voice heard.
- The 10 commandments of effective networking:
  - You get what you give.
  - Be yourself.
  - Honour your relationships.
  - Share; don't hoard.
  - Ask for what you want.
  - Promote yourself professionally.
  - Move on when necessary.
  - Record all your contacts.
  - Follow up.
  - Expand your horizons.

Appendix
Where to go from here

Communication is continuous, and we never finish learning how to improve. My blog explores issues and events relating to the material in this book. You can find it at: bit.ly/1zgJBvo.

Here are some thoughts about books and other resources that will take further the ideas we have explored in this book.

Chapter 1: What is communication?

The fullest explanation I have found of the Shannon–Weaver model of communication is on Mick Underwood's magnificent (and award-winning) website: bit.ly/29CaP7Q.

The four principles of communication are based on ideas by Donnell King. Find them at: bit.ly/1NfLVmS.

Chris Dyas explains his five steps to building rapport here: bit.ly/29xhu5U.

The Wikipedia article on Paul Watzlawick provides useful information and links.

If you want to go further, Steven Mithen's book *The Prehistory of the Mind* (Phoenix, London, 1998) discusses the origins of communication in primate activity. Margaret Wheatley's *Leadership and the New Science* (Berret-Koehler, San Francisco, CA, 1992) brings insights from quantum theory and complexity to bear on ideas of information.

Chapter 2: How conversations work

Find out more about Paul Grice's maxims of conversation here: bit.ly/1Q91bXi.

And you can find amusing demonstrations of all four maxims taken from *The Big Bang Theory* here: bit.ly/1OrMEp2.

French and Raven's five bases of power are well explained here: bit.ly/1ZvFOlo.

Peter Senge's book *The Fifth Discipline* (Random House, London, 2nd edn, 2006) relates conversation to systems theory. William Isaac's *Dialogue and the Art of Thinking Together* (Currency Books, New York, 1999) is at the leading edge of studies into conversation.

Chapter 3: Seven ways to improve your conversations

First- and second-stage thinking are notions that inform Edward de Bono's work. Look at *Lateral Thinking in Management* (Penguin, London, 1982). The four types of conversation derive from the work of Michael Wallacek, who may have been influenced by Werner Erhard.

Chris Argyris's ladder of inference is best found in *The Fifth Discipline Fieldbook*, edited by Peter Senge and others (Nicholas Brealey, London, 1994).

For more on mind maps, see Tony Buzan's *Use your Head* (BBC, London, 1974).

Chapter 4: The skills of enquiry

Nancy Kline's *Time to Think* (Ward Lock, London, 1999) is a fascinating study of deep listening.

Chapter 5: The skills of persuasion

Aristotle explains his three modes of appeal in *The Art of Rhetoric* (Penguin Classics, London, 1991).

A warrant is a key component of a Toulmin schema, developed by the philosopher Stephen Toulmin. Find out more here: bit.ly/1U6GX1y.

Caroline Goyder includes her ideas on voice production in her book *Gravitas* (Vermilion, London, 2014).

Peter Thompson's *Persuading Aristotle* (Kogan Page, London, 1999) entertainingly relates classical rhetoric to modern business techniques.

For more on pyramids, look at Barbara Minto's *The Pyramid Principle* (Pitman, London, 1987).

Chapter 6: Tough conversations

Find out how well Paul McLean's model of the triune brain is surviving:

- bit.ly/1PaQK8G.
- bit.ly/1PB8vID.

I draw on the work of Joe Griffin and Ivan Tyrrell in this chapter and elsewhere in this book. You can research their work by going to the Human Givens Institute website (hgi.org.uk). Find out more about the limbic system here: bit.ly/29HkLz9.

Explore our needs as human beings here: bit.ly/29xg4mm.

And you can take an online emotional needs audit here: bit.ly/29xg1at.

Chapter 7: Making a presentation

You can find a worked example of Monroe's motivated sequence here: bit.ly/1ndUE4m.

PRAISE is based loosely on the material in *Made to Stick* by Chip and Dan Heath (Arrow, London, 2008).

Jens Kjeldsen has analysed slide usage in his paper, The Rhetoric of PowerPoint: bit.ly/209vX7d.

Max Atkinson's book *Lend Me Your Ears* (Vermilion, London, 2004) takes a strikingly new approach to the subject of presenting and speech writing.

Chapter 8: Putting it in writing

Justin Kruger's paper on e-mail's potential for misunderstandings is here: bit.ly/SyB0jo.

Kristin Byron's article, Carrying Too Heavy a Load?, is available here: bit.ly/1OrR5QJ.

Jay Heinrichs talks about the tenses of persuasion in his book *Thank You for Arguing* (Three Rivers Press, New York, 2013).

Alan Barker's *Writing at Work* (Industrial Society, London, 1999) is a comprehensive guide to writing business documents.

Chapter 9: Networking

Two books taking usefully complementary approaches to networking are Steven D'Souza's *Brilliant Networking* (Pearson Education, Harlow, 2008), and *Power Networking* by Donna Fisher and Sandy Vilas (Bard Press, Atlanta, GA, USA, 2000).

Creating Success Series

The above titles are available from all good bookshops.

For further information on these and other Kogan Page titles, or to order online, visit the Kogan Page website at: **www.koganpage.com**.